THE MANUAL OF PHOTO-TECHNIQUE

THE MANUAL

OF PHOTO-TECHNIQUE

EXPOSURE
By W. F. Berg, D.Sc., Ph.D., F.R.P.S.

OPTICS
By Arthur Cox, B.Sc., M.A.

ENLARGING
By C. I. Jacobson, Ph.D.

DEVELOPING
By C. I. Jacobson, Ph.D.

ILLUMINATION
By R. H. Cricks, F.R.P.S., F.B.K.S.

RETOUCHING
By O. R. Croy, Ph.D.

Edited by A. KRASZNA-KRAUSZ

RETOUCHING

CORRECTIVE TECHNIQUES IN PHOTOGRAPHY

By O. R. CROY, Ph.D.

THE FOCAL PRESS

LONDON and NEW YORK

ALL INQUIRIES

relating to this book or to any other photographic problem are readily answered by the Focal Press and its Circle of Photographers without charge if a stamped addressed envelope is enclosed for reply and the inquiry sent to

FOCAL PRESS, 31 FITZROY SQUARE, LONDON, W.1

Printed 1953 in Great Britain by W. & J. Mackay & Co., Ltd., Chatham, for The Focal Press Ltd., Fitzroy Square, London, W.1.

Technique is as much subject to snobbisms as most other fields of human activity. The artist for whom all Art must be handmade is matched by the photographer who will not tolerate handwork in a photograph.

The sober truth is that, with photography being put to increasingly diversified uses and large prints continuing to be made from ever smaller negatives, the need for correctives—whether they be manual or semi-manual—is to-day as great as ever. On the whole photographers may be spending—mainly for economic reasons—less of their time on the facial rejuvenation of their clients than they used to but skilled professional retouchers still cannot complain of under-employment.

Professional retouchers, however, are, as a rule, more articulate with their hands than in the literary sense. O. R. Croy belongs to the very few who are both competent and exceptionally qualified to explain the simple but subtle manual techniques on which photographic retouching depends.

It is over seventeen years ago that I persuaded him to undertake this work but the war and its aftermath have retarded the incorporation of his slim volume in the " Manual of Photo-Technique " series. For this series the original manuscript was carefully revised, the illustrative material greatly expanded and new diagrammatic representations evolved to analyse and recapitulate the sequences of all operations.

A. KRASZNA-KRAUSZ

Most of the illustrations were taken by the author. Outside contributors include the following :

S. Enkelmann   (p. 21)
Max Factor   (pp. 26–29)
Walter Nurnberg   (pp. 17–19, 85, 96 bottom, and 97 top right)
A. Thévenet   (p. 20)

CONTENTS

WHY RETOUCHING ?
    Retouching is an End   13

POINTS OF PREVENTION
    Care and Cleanliness   15
    Precaution Against Damage   16
    Photographic Technique   49
    Soft-Focus Lenses   49
    Make-up   50
    Other Methods   51

A SYSTEM OF RETOUCHING
    Order of Operations   54

CHEMICAL RETOUCHING
    Working Position   56
    Reduction   58
    Reducing the Centre of a Negative   58
    Sharp Outlines   59
    Resist Masks   60
    Unsharp Outlines   60
    Intensification   62

THE RETOUCHING DESK
    Retouching by Daylight   65
    Retouching by Artificial Light   65
    The Ground Glass   68
    Correct Posture   69

DYE AND PIGMENT RETOUCHING
    Holding Back   70
    Equipment   70
    Applying the Dye   72
    Judging the Effect   73
    Dyeing by Immersion   73
    Spotting   74
    Dye and Pigment Media   74
    The Brush   78
    Spotting with Dye   80
    Spotting with Pigment   80

ABRASIVE RETOUCHING

Stumps	106
Abrasive Powders and Pastes	108
Applying the Abrasive	110
Knifework	111
The Right Knife	111
Sharpening	112
Stropping	114
The Correct Stroke	115
Removing Spots and Lines	116
Roughening the Surface	116
Enlarging Negatives after Knifework	116

PENCIL RETOUCHING

The Need for Retouching	118
Freckles and Eye Shadows	119
Psychological Factors	120
Preliminary Varnishing	120
Types of Varnish	120
Choice of Pencil	126
Matching Density	127
The Correct Pencil Stroke	127
Sharpening the Point	127
Faults and Failures	128

RETOUCHING ON THE BACK

Matt Varnish	129
Holding Back with Graphite	130
Holding Back with Pigment	131
Blocking Out	132
Softening the Outline	132
Preparing a Dye Border	134
Filling in the Background	134

DAMAGED NEGATIVES

Dealing with Scratches	136
Broken Plates	138

MINIATURE NEGATIVES

Essential Equipment	140
Work on the Negative	141
Suppressing Grain	141
Soft-Focus Methods	142
Making a Duplicate	144
Redevelopment	144

PRINT RETOUCHING

After-treatment of Prints	154
Removing Stains	156
Dry Retouching on Prints	157
Matt Surfaces	157

Retouching for Reproduction 158
Semi-Matt Prints 159
Glossy Surfaces 160
Varnishing Prints 161
Spray Varnishing 163
Spraying Matt 163
Tinting 164

AIR BRUSHING 165

Air Brushes 166
Pressure Supply 166
Air Brush Colours 168
Working Procedure 178
Close Spraying 178
Tone Control 179
Masking 179
Cutting the Mask 180
Spraying with the Mask 181
Multiple Masks 182
Soft Outlines 182
Spraying Clouds 182
Dealing with Mistakes 183
Cleaning after Use

RESTORING DAMAGED PICTURES 185

Stains 186
Water Spots 186
Old and Varnished Negatives 187
Restoring Prints 188
Faded Prints

9

LIST OF FORMULAE

1. Farmer's Reducer 58
2. Ferric Oxalate Reducer 60
3. Potassium Ferricyanide Reducer 62
4. Copper Intensifier 64
5. Chromium Intensifier 64
6. Liquid Filter 68
7. Dry Reducer 108
8. Alternative Dry Reducer 108
9. Abrasive Medium 110
10. Water Varnish 122
11. Warm Alcohol Varnish for Plates 122
12. Cold Varnish 122
13. Alternative Cold Varnish 122
14. Normal Matting Varnish 123
15. Rapid Matting Varnish 123
16. Matt Varnish for Plates 130
17. Alternative Matt Varnish 130
18. Bleaching Bath 153
19. Redeveloper for Fine Grain 153
20. Potassium Permanganate Reducer 156
21. Thiocarbamide Clearing Bath 156
22. Wax Polish for Prints 162
23. Glossy Varnish 162
24. Semi-matt Varnish 162
25. Starch Solution 163
26. Air Brush Masking Varnish 181
27. Stain Remover 185
28. Alternative Stain Remover 185
29. First Bleaching Bath 186
30. Second Bleaching Bath 186
31. Clearing Bath 186
32. Iodine Bleacher 187
33. Bichromate Bleacher 188
34. Copper Sulphate Bleacher 188
35. Metol-Hydroquinone Developer 188

LIST OF TABLES

I	Max Factor Panchromatic Make-Up	50
II	Leichner Panchromatic Make-up	50
III	Retouching Dyes, Pigments and Opaques	75
IV	Varnishes and Retouching Media	124
V	Retouching Pencils	126

WHY RETOUCHING?

There are two schools of thought about photographic retouching. Some people consider it a necessity, others hold that it can be dispensed with. There may be something to be said for both views, if they refer to one particular photograph ; but photographers would be seriously handicapped if retouching were abolished altogether.

There are many unexpected snags that may crop up in the various processes of photography. In fact, the production of photographs would shrink to a fraction of its present volume if only unretouched negatives and prints were generally acceptable.

Let us suppose that, in spite of all our care, a bit of material chips off the inside of the camera and, falling on the negative emulsion, causes a black spot. If we do not believe in retouching, we may perhaps be able to take the photograph again, when, of course, no retouching will be needed. But what if the material chips off and spoils a negative that cannot be repeated ? There is nothing for it but to accept the inevitable and have the spot removed by retouching.

Retouching is an End

Retouching must of course be invisible, for it is only a corrective process ; the work must be made to blend with the character of the photograph.

A good deal of experience is needed for really invisible retouching. Failing this experience—and those who do not believe in retouching are unlikely to have it—an attempt at retouching may make the fault even worse. But with practice we can actually learn to improve the photograph ; and overcome our antipathy to the process.

To get a good print, we must have a good negative. But no matter how original the subject or treatment, the print can be ruined by careless presentation. Careful retouching is often necessary with unusual subjects which tax our equipment to the utmost and (in the event of success), raise the work above the common mean.

It would clearly be a mistake to pass a subject by for fear of being obliged to resort to retouching to remove some minor but unavoidable defect. It would also be wrong to alter the over-all lighting of a subject which is otherwise satisfactory because of a single unsightly shadow in one place. The shadow is easily eliminated by moving the lamps, but at the same time the over-all effect is lost. It may be therefore better to leave the lamps as they are and remove the small shadow later by retouching.

We shall describe all methods of retouching, with special emphasis on those which permit a reasonable degree of enlargement. While the older techniques are mentioned, prominence is given to the latest methods which satisfy the requirements of advanced workers.

Whatever the method, it is the result that counts, and as in all other photographic processes, personal preference plays a large part in determining the when and how of retouching. But the aim should always be to achieve such skill in retouching that it never occurs to anyone looking at the print to inquire whether it was, in fact, retouched !

POINTS OF PREVENTION

Retouching is in effect a process of cleaning up afterwards—after taking the picture, developing the negative, or after making the print.

In retouching, as in any other craft concerned with putting things right, timely prevention saves a great deal of curing.

Care and Cleanliness

The most common defects requiring retouching are spots and lines due to dust and to damage—scratches and the like.

Therefore keep all equipment clean and free of dust. This applies to the camera and negative material as well as to the processing solutions. Filter the developer before use, particularly if it is a solution freshly made up from solid chemicals. Give the films or plates a final rinse in water with wetting agent added to avoid drying marks.

Obviously the place where the negatives are dried should be free of dust, too. As, however, no room is ever absolutely dust-free, the main aim is to avoid stirring up the dust which is everywhere. Settled dust is harmless. So keep out draughts and don't walk about near drying negatives.

Even dry films may get dusty, though the dust can then be removed. They must therefore be cleaned just before enlarging or printing. But excessive vigour in cleaning may achieve exactly the opposite to the desired result. Vigorous rubbing induces an electric charge on the films and plates, and they then actually attract the dust suspended in the air. Therefore wipe the negatives clean slowly.

15

After drying, plates and 35 mm. films (which have no gelatine backing layer) may show traces of dried-up drops of water on the back, particularly if the washing water was hard. To remove these, put the negative face down on a clean sheet of paper. Breathe on the back, and polish with a soft piece of chamois leather or a piece of cotton wool. Repeat and continue until further breathing on the back shows no more traces of the deposit.

Negatives just cleaned should not be enlarged straight away. The electric charge produced by rubbing must be given a chance to disappear, which will take a few minutes. Then put them in the enlarger after careful final dusting. That should be done with dry hands. However dry the hand is, traces of moisture will still cling to it, and these will help to take the dust with them. So wipe over the plates gently with the palm of the hand, or in the case of films pull them slowly through between the second and third fingers.

Even if the negative is now free of dust, the glass plates of the negative carrier—if the carrier has glass plates—are by no means clean yet. Here again, breathe on them and gently polish with a piece of wash-leather before putting in the negative. It is always better to be too meticulous than not painstaking enough when dealing with dust.

Precautions against Damage

Handle negatives carefully all the time to avoid injury. Make a habit of only holding them by the edges, and even there only with two fingers.

Fingerprints on the film are easily avoided by careful handling. Moist fingerprints are particularly dangerous. If we notice them immediately, no harm is done, but the negative must straight away be soaked in water and dried again.

The same applies to water splashes on the gelatine. Once these have dried in, not much can be done. Sometimes, but only rarely, weak ammonia solution may help :

AVOIDING RETOUCHING. We can take steps even before making an exposure. In this case, toning down the hard features of the portrait may require quite a lot of handwork.

SOFT FOCUS. Printing the negative through a diffusing screen softens the outlines and detail (p. 49) to produce a more pleasant result. The effect is obtained by the shadow areas of the image spreading into the highlights.

A soft focus lens on the camera softens the image, but in a different way. The spreading of light takes place during the original exposure. As a result, the highlights spread into the shadows to yield a hazy, luminous effect.

On pages 20–21 : CHOICE OF LIGHTING. Harsh and brilliant direct lighting brings out every pore, every hair and every spot on the face (p. 20). That is suitable for character faces as in this case, but would need an enormous amount of retouching in straight portraiture. Softer lighting (p. 21) keeps the skin texture smooth and reduces the need for retouching.

CHOICE OF FILM. Freckles and similar pigmentation flaws show up strongly on ortho film which is insensitive to red (*opposite*). Fully colour sensitive panchromatic materials subdue the skin blemishes, but also tend to make lips too light (*above*) which therefore require special make-up. Orthochromatic films are satisfactory for portraiture only with clear-skinned subjects.

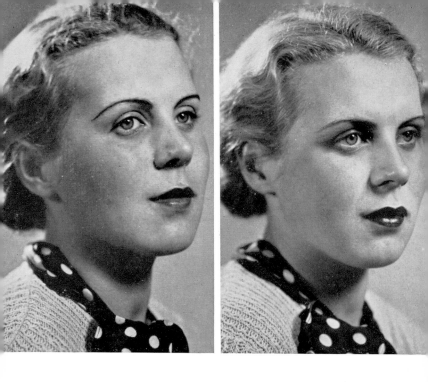

ORTHOCHROMATIC FILM AND MAKE-UP. Even with ortho film make-up can improve the face (*left*) by covering up freckles, clearing up and accentuating the lip line. Eye shadow makes the eyes look less bulging (*right*).

PANCHROMATIC FILM AND MAKE-UP. For artificial light portraiture on pan materials, especially the highly red-sensitive types, make-up is almost indispensable. This yields the best possible tone reproduction (*right*). Without make-up (*left*) the lips appear excessively pale.

THE SCOPE OF MAKE-UP. In modern photographic studios make-up technique has taken an enormous amount of work out of the retoucher's hands. In motion picture production where retouching is completely out of question, make-up was perfected to a fine art. It can, in fact, turn a perfectly plain face (*above*) into a glamour portrait (*opposite*).

On pages 28-29: MAKE-UP TECHNIQUE. A complete make-up scheme to achieve a really professional result starts with a suitable foundation on which highlights, shadows and eyeshadow are applied. That is then followed by eyebrow pencil, eye-lash and lip treatment, and finally by rouge (see p. 50).

MAKE-UP STAGES. *Top right :* Applying the foundation. *Below left :* Applying eye shadow. After the foundation and shadow colours are dry, they should be powdered over, and the surplus brushed off. *Below right :* Lining the eyebrows with eyebrow pencil.

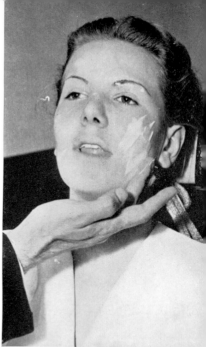

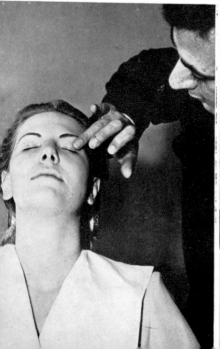

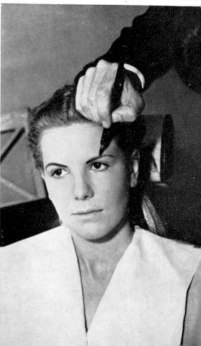

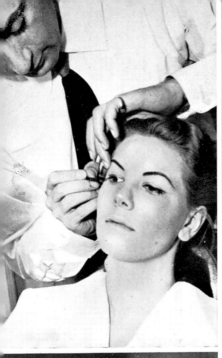

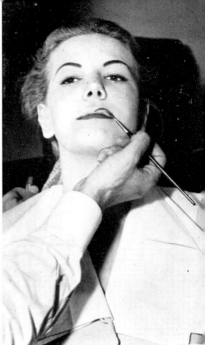

Top left : Applying eye-lash make-up. *Top right :* Using lipstick. This is best painted on to produce a more even effect—painting also gives greater control over the outlines. *Bottom left :* Brushing on rouge.

THE SCOPE OF RETOUCHING. The crosses indicate the points most likely to need attention ; wrinkles in the hands, around the mouth, neck and the eyes, and shadows by the mouth. Most of these

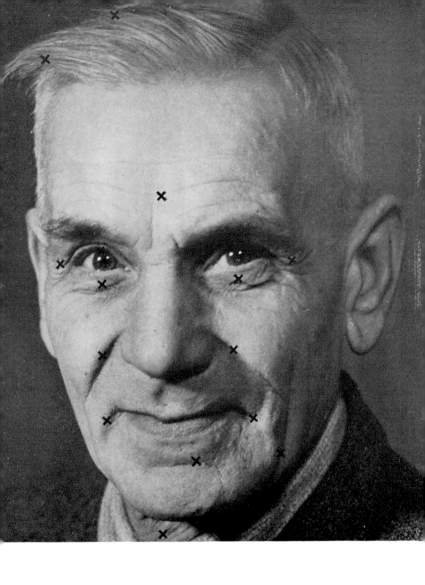

can be dealt with by pencil retouching (p. 118). With older men (*above*)
it is generally better not to retouch facial features as would be necessary
on a portrait of a younger person.

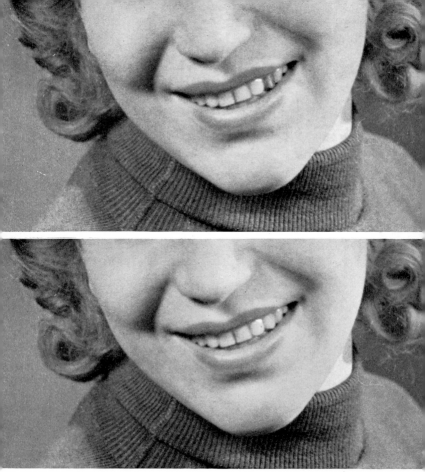

THE TEETH. Gold fillings and gold crowns may mar the appearance of the mouth (*top*) as they appear darker than the surrounding teeth. The best way is to hold back the area on the negative (*bottom*) by means of grey or red retouching dye (p. 20).

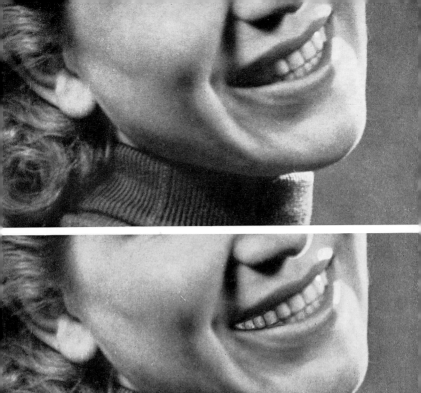

MOUTH SHADOWS. Where part of the mouth is in shadow (*top*), the missing detail of the corners of the mouth and teeth (*below*) can be painted in with pigment (p. 74) or retouched in with pencil (p. 118).

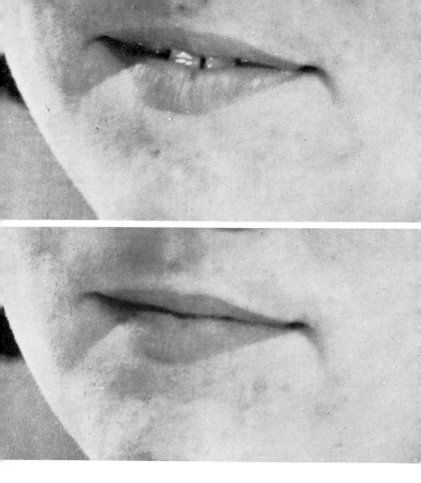

THE LIP LINE. Unflattering lips (*top*) can be corrected by scraping with the knife (p. 111) to take out the highlights and visible detail of the teeth, followed by touching up by pencil (*bottom*) to match the tone with the surrounding area.

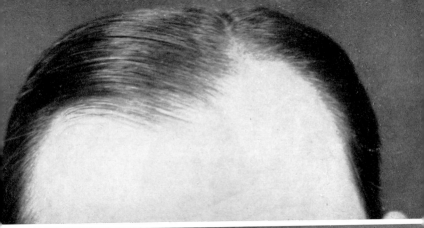

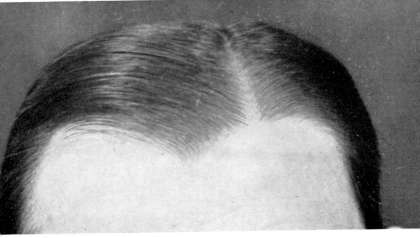

THE HAIR LINE. The forehead may need rejuvenation (*top*), either by scraping hairs on to the head (*bottom*) in the negative, or drawing them in pencil on the print (p. 158). Do not add too much hair, or it will look like a wig.

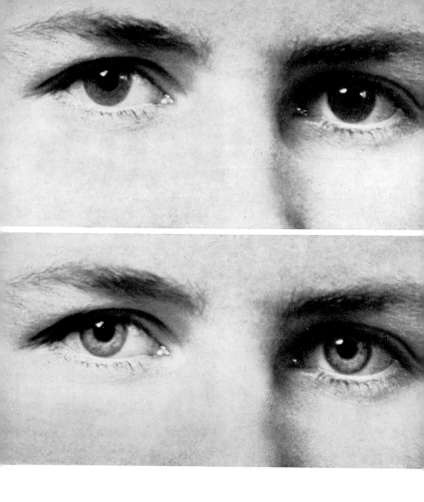

THE EYES. Brown or deep blue eyes may reproduce too dark in artificial light (*top*). Here the iris needs holding back by carefully painting the area with a suitable dye (p. 70) to give the eyes more life (*bottom*).

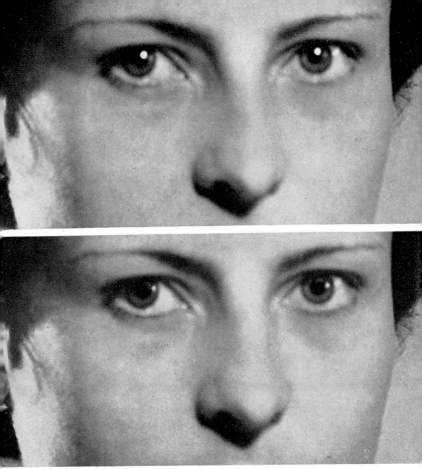

CATCHLIGHTS. In the pupil of the eye catchlights produce a staring expression (*top*). We can remove it by knifing out the catchlight on the negative (p. 111), and inserting a new spot in the right place (*bottom*) with the retouching pencil (p. 118).

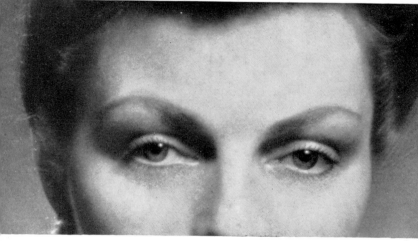

EYELASHES. Where eyelashes are indistinct (*top*), they can be reinforced or inserted on the negative by knifing (p. 111). The eye shadows may also be subdued by pencil retouching (*bottom*).

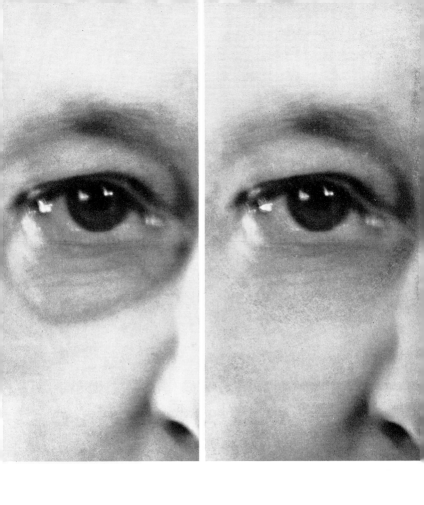

EYE SHADOWS. Deep shadows, particularly rings under the eyes, make a face look tired and old (*left*). They are best pencilled out on the negative (p. 118) or held back with dye (*right*).

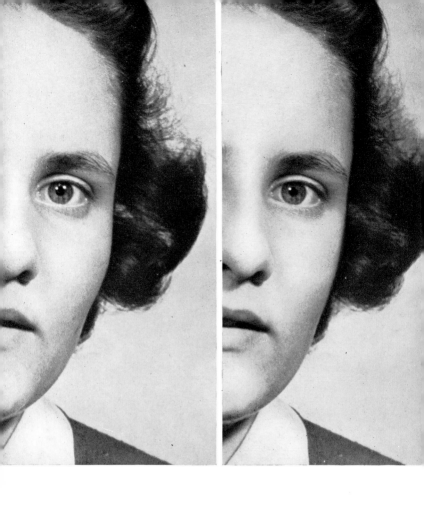

THE HAIR AND CHEEK BONES. Black retouching dye, applied to the print (p. 157) may be used to clean up untidy hair (*left*) and also, as in this case, correct too prominent cheek bones (*right*).

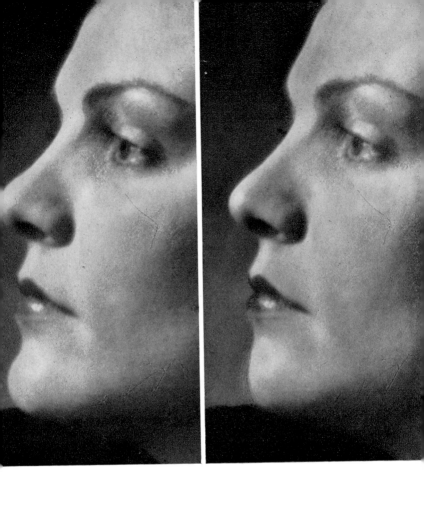

THE SHAPE OF THE CHIN. A jutting out chin (*left*) is easily altered by careful knifing on the negative or by the use of retouching dye on the print (*right*).

THE NOSE. To change the nose, it is best to modify the relative
masses of light and shade on it. By a decrease in the highlight area (with
dye on the print) a broad fleshy nose (*above*) becomes distinctly

narrower (*above*). The retouched area must blend in completely with
the shadow density of the image which is most successfully achieved by
applying washes of dilute dye.

THE FOREHEAD. The lines on the forehead (*above*) though often caused by frowning, are also a sign of age and will not flatter a portrait.

Pencil work on the negative (p. 118) will subdue the furrows and smooth the skin (*above*).

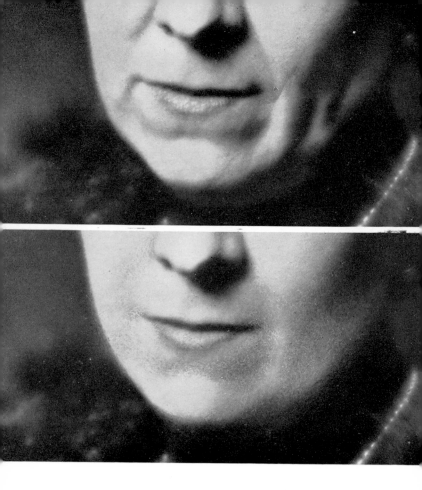

WRINKLES. Folds and wrinkles (*top*) often need a great deal of pencil work and account for most of the rejuvenation entrusted to retouchers. When eliminating wrinkles be careful not to falsify the anatomical structure of the face ; the main shadows, though subdued, must still be there to retain modelling (*bottom*).

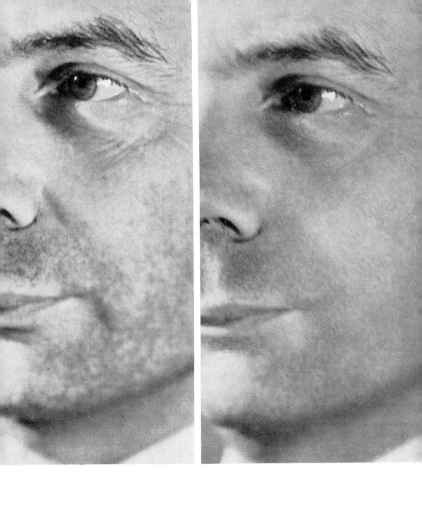

BEARD SHADOW. On an unshaven chin (*left*) the stubbles have to be blended into the skin tone with the retouching pencil. Generally, larger areas that are not sharp enough to show the individual hairs can be held back with dye on the negative (p. 70) to lighten the beard shadow (*right*).

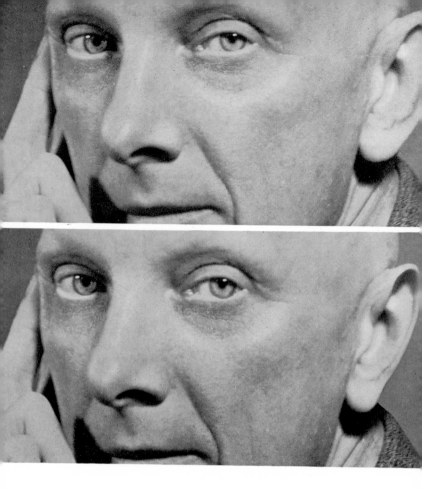

THE EARS. Protruding ears (*top*) and similar anatomical corrections call for more advanced changes. In this case (*bottom*) the ear was re-painted on the print with pigment (p. 158) and the background then air brushed to make it even (p. 165). Usually it is advisable to rephotograph the print if several copies are required.

soak the negatives for a few hours in water with a few drops of ammonia added, then dry without further washing.

Greasy finger-prints are fairly easily removed by polishing the negative with a piece of cotton wool soaked in carbon tetrachloride or trichloroethylene. Better still, wash the hands before handling negatives !

To preserve them in storage put them into thin translucent envelopes which will best protect them against scratches and other marks.

Photographic Technique

We can also avoid, or at least reduce, the retouching required at the end by selecting the right films and equipment *before* the exposure. It is often a question of taking appropriate steps to compensate for the known limitations of certain emulsions.

For instance orthochromatic film will exaggerate skin blemishes when exposed by arc light, and retouching is then necessary to remove them. But with panchromatic film and Photoflood lamps, the blemishes disappear. At the same time, however, the model's lips, the colour of which approximates to that of the blemishes, are rendered too light. A pale green filter will give a correct rendering of the lips, but will also bring out the blemishes again.

There are two ways out of this dilemma : using a soft-focus lens, or appropriate make-up.

Soft-Focus Lenses

These lenses produce a slightly unsharp image superimposed on a sharp one. The general effect is one of softened definition with consequent loss of the finest detail, including the skin blemishes.

We can also obtain a soft-focus image with a normal lens by using a soft focus attachment (e.g., Duto, Modulo, Rolleisoft) or exposing through a sheet of gauze, crepe georgette or similar muslin-like fabric.

Besides the loss of detail, the effect of depth is enhanced.

R.—B   49

Photographs taken with a diffusing medium are therefore immediately distinguishable from those taken without such aids.

Make-up

Photographic make-up can hide many facial imperfections. In its simplest form, to eliminate skin blemishes, we can suitably darken the model's lips, and make the exposure on panchromatic film without a filter.

Several types of photographic make-up are available for more advanced work.

I—MAX FACTOR PANCHROMATIC MAKE-UP

Make-up	Women	Men
Foundation	Pan-Cake N5 or 25	Pan-Cake N8 or 28
Highlights	Pan-Cake N2 or 21	Pan-Cake N5 or 25
Shadows	Pan-Cake N8 or 28	Pan-Cake N11
Powder	25 or 1A	(None)
Eyeshadow liner	6 or 21	6 (if necessary)
Eyebrow pencil	Brown or black	Brown or black
Moist rouge	No. 2 or 390A	2 or 8 Pancro
Dry rouge (if used)	Light Tech.	Dark Tech.
Eyelash make-up	Brownish black or black	(None)

II—LEICHNER PANCHROMATIC MAKE-UP

Make-up	Women	Men
Foundation	Allcromo A 101, 102, 103	Allcromo A 105, 106, 108, 110
Shadows	A 127 (light)	A 127 (dark), A 122
Eyeshadow	Form E (silver blue, silver lilac)	Form E 31 (pale grey), E 32 (dark grey)
Highlights	Form E 22 (white)	Form E 22 (white)
Eyebrow pencil	Ultra Dermatograph Type 46 (black, brown, light brown, grey)	Ultra Dermatograph Type 46 (black, brown, light brown, grey)
Powder	Type 230a (yellowish pink, brownish)	Type 230a (yellowish pink, brownish)
	Yellowish natural	Okre Rose
	Type 102 (invisible powder) yellowish pink natural	Okre Orient
	Flesh colour	Flesh colour
Lipstick or paint	Stick : No. 1037 Paint : 64/20	Stick : No. 1037 Paint : 64/20

Other Methods

A polarizing filter (e.g., Zeiss Bernotar, Kodak Pola-Filter) provides a further means of what we may call *optical retouching*. It will cut out unwanted reflections such as occur on spectacle lenses, and render subsequent retouching unnecessary.

We can, of course, avoid much subsequent retouching by control of the lighting. Soft diffused light gives far less prominence to surface detail than the hard, concentrated illumination characteristic of spotlights.

Vignetting effects can also be achieved during the original exposure. The method consists of placing a suitable cut-out mask of paper or gauze about 2 feet in front of the lens. The picture then shows an unsharp image of the mask, which either hides or diffuses the detail behind it.

In special fields, such as copying, infra-red film is useful for dealing with faded, dirty, or stained documents and drawings. This eliminates many of the stains and makes retouching unnecessary.

To handle these various methods successfully, we must have an adequate knowledge of retouching processes and their effects. It is not sufficient to know how to use soft-focus lenses and colour and polarizing filters for routine purposes. Over and above this knowledge, we need an understanding of the special applications of these devices for our purposes to reduce the retouching.

The fact, for instance, that a soft-focus lens gives a diffused image is of secondary importance ; what we are concerned with is the elimination of fine detail, and thus of skin blemishes.

The solutions for chemical treatment are :

R. = reducer
In. = intensifier
S.B.= stop bath
F. = fixing bath
C. = clearing bath
Dv. = developer

The spotting and retouching materials are :

D. = retouching dye
G. = gum (for glossy prints)
I. = Indian ink

You also need varnishes :

V. = negative varnishes
M.V.= matt varnish

Retouching media also come into this category.

For retouching you will need various materials and solutions which are indicated in the diagrams of this book by the symbols and letters shown here.

From *top* to *bottom* cotton wool, blotting paper, oil, a soft rag, abrasive medium, pumice powder, water colour and a supply of clean water.

Useful solvents (for washing off varnish resists, etc.) include :

P. = petrol
A. = alcohol
T. = turpentine

RETOUCHING ORDER

1. The first stage in retouching is chemical treatment which involves immersing parts of the image in solutions such as reducers to lighten, and intensifiers to darken, the image (p. 56).

2. Next comes dye retouching and holding back. Red or grey retouching dyes are used to darken areas of the negative in order to make them print lighter (p. 70).

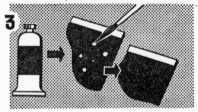

3. For clear spots in very dense areas, water colour pigment is better than dye since you can build up greater densities more quickly (p. 80).

4. Black spots and similar flaws are best removed by scraping with a knife (p. 111).

5. Pencil retouching, preceded by an application of varnish to enable the surface to take the pencil, is used to modify individual features, e.g., of the face (p. 118).

A SYSTEM OF RETOUCHING

The first essential in negative retouching is to work to a system. If a negative requires several different kinds of treatment, the various retouching methods here described should be applied in an order in which no new treatment interferes with work already completed.

Beginners are specially advised to observe this order, as they will then be in a position to correct any mistakes they may make without damage to the negative.

Order of Operations

Chemical treatment—reduction or intensification—follows logically on normal negative processing, and is carried out on the negative when wet. Though we are here only concerned with treatment of a part of the negative, this process clearly comes first. All subsequent retouching methods are carried out on the dry negative.

Dye retouching comes next. Dye is applied with a brush to the thinner parts of the negative that print too dark. Mistakes can be corrected by simply washing the dye away and making a fresh start.

Spotting is the next step, and here again mistakes can be removed by a further rinse.

If all has gone well, we may now start with *mechanical or frictional reduction*. This is an abrasive removal of density from fairly large areas. It requires more caution as mistakes can no longer be so easily rectified.

Knifing with a special knife is the next process. Its purpose is to lighten details of the negative which are too dense, or to remove the image altogether. As the emulsion is damaged in the process, it is inadvisable to attempt to remove mistakes by rinsing the negative afterwards as can be safely done after dye retouching or spotting. This is why, as already mentioned, the latter methods must come first.

The final stage of negative treatment is *pencil retouching*. A layer of varnish is first applied to the emulsion. No brush work, spotting or etching is possible on the varnished surface, which is also impervious to water, so that rinsing does not affect it.

It is specially important to adhere to the above order of operations when retouching plates. The order can be varied with double-coated films, as both layers are available for retouching. This does not, however, apply to films with matt backing, or to miniature films, both of which should be treated strictly in the sequence described.

CHEMICAL RETOUCHING

Chemical after-treatment of negatives by reduction or intensification will sometimes improve a picture. This is, in fact, part of the negative technique, and may rectify faults like excessive or insufficient density and contrast. For retouching we can apply these methods locally to selected areas of the image. The processes differ very little from general reduction and intensification. While over-all chemical treatment influences the character of the whole negative, we are only concerned to treat part of it.

In consequence, we cannot place the film or plate in an appropriate bath, as all the silver deposit would be affected. We must take steps to limit the chemical influence to certain portions only of the negative. Though not unduly difficult, this work does call for a certain amount of skill.

We need the following implements :

One small and one large brush, with very soft bristles (a quill handle is preferable to metal or wood) ;

A dropping tube ;

Some cotton wool ;

A sheet of photographic blotting paper ;

A glass dish with transparent bottom (a plain sheet of glass will serve equally well).

Working Position

It is best to work near a window and to arrange a reflecting surface so that, with the plate held horizontally, the light shines up through it. The easiest way is to place a large white dish on a table and hold the negative above it.

It is an advantage to have a sprinkler handy, but if none is available, place a second dish of clean water ready.

LOCAL REDUCTION

To apply reducer to parts of the negative you will need a dropping tube, one or two brushes, blotting paper and a sheet of glass. To judge the effect on the negative, hold it against a white surface with plenty of light falling on it (*right*).

To reduce, say, an over-dense sky, proceed as follows (p. 58).

1. Soak the negative in water for ten minutes.

2. Hold it over the dish of reducer.

3. Soak a ball of cotton wool in the reducer.

4. Let the reducer flow over the area to be reduced. Tilt the negative so that the solution drains off at one corner. Follow the outlines as accurately as possible.

5. Wipe the cotton wool over the parts under treatment occasionally to make sure that the reducer is evenly distributed.

6. Finally wash the negative well in running water.

Left : Film negatives are not so easy to handle, therefore mount them on a sheet of plate glass with rubber cement.

Right : To reduce an area in the centre of the negative apply the solution with a dropping tube (p. 83).

Reduction

To take a typical case, let us suppose that we have a negative of a landscape that is correctly exposed except for the sky. The latter is so dense that the clouds do not print at all. Reduction of the sky is indicated, but the effect must not be allowed to extend to other parts of the negative.

First rinse the negative for about ten minutes to make the gelatine layer swell. Then, holding the negative at a slant over the white dish, the foreground upwards, the sky downwards, let the water run off into the white dish.

Next take a swab of cotton wool soaked in Farmer's reducer and squeeze it over the sky area of the negative. Make sure that the reducer flows in a thin trickle along the edge of the landscape and spreads evenly over the sky ; also that the plate is inclined correctly to assist the flow. Now and then gently pass the cotton wool itself over the sky, but avoid applying any pressure.

I.—FARMER'S REDUCER

A.	Potassium ferricyanide	88 grains	5 grams
	Water	4 ounces	100 c.cm.
B.	Sodium thiosulphate (hypo)	88 grains	5 grams
	Water	4 ounces	100 c.cm.

For use mix 1 part of solution B with 4 parts of solution A. This mixture does not keep for more than about $\frac{1}{4}$ hour ; make it up immediately before it is needed.

The weaker the solution, the less danger of uneven reduction. We can avoid it altogether by frequent sprinkling of the plate or rinsing in the plain water dish. If the sky area is small, or the negative is a miniature one, the reducer is best applied by the dropping tube instead of cotton wool.

When working on a film, lay it emulsion side upwards on a wet glass plate. It will adhere there and can be treated just like a plate negative.

Reducing the Centre of a Negative

Local reduction is rather more difficult if the part of the negative to be treated lies in the middle. The reducer cannot be poured on and allowed to flow away, as it would then affect adjacent parts which we do not want to reduce.

The reducer works most strongly at the point of first application and progressively loses strength as it flows down the plate. If we therefore keep the plate in constant motion after applying the reducer, the solution will flow over different parts.

Thus while the edges of the negative will be affected to a certain extent, reduction will not be as strong as in the centre.

The best way to obtain an even result is to keep turning the negative while applying the reducer to the centre, so that the reducer flows across a different part of the edge each time. Frequent sprinkling or rinsing of the negative between applications of reducer is also recommended.

Sharp Outlines

The work becomes more intricate when a sharp outline must be followed, as for instance when reducing an over-exposed window in an interior scene.

Working methods vary according to whether the outline must be precisely followed, or slight overlapping is permissible or necessary.

In the former case, support each end of the dry plate (or film laid on a sheet of glass) on a book or small box after the fashion of a bridge. Then place a sheet of white paper below the plate. The white surface acts as a background against which to observe the work.

Apply the reducer with a brush, exactly following the outline in question, and keep the solution moving so as to ensure even reduction.

If the brush passes beyond the line, mop up the surplus reducer with a corner of blotting paper. Wipe the area at once with a second brush dipped in plain water, which should be ready to hand. As it takes some time to spread the reducer over the whole surface, it is advisable to use a very weak solution.

The potassium ferric oxalate reducer is particularly suitable for this method as it works considerably more slowly than Farmer's formula. A fair amount of skill is required to apply the reducer evenly and rapidly to the whole surface.

2.—FERRIC OXALATE REDUCER

Ferric potassium oxalate	35 grains	2 grams
Sodium thiosulphate	265 grains	15 grams
Water to make	4 ounces	100 c.cm.

Resist Masks

Failing this ability good results can be obtained by first carefully painting a waterproof coat over those parts of the negative that are not to be reduced. The purpose of the coating is to protect the appropriate areas from the action of the reducer, yet to come off easily after treatment.

A suitable resist medium is asphalt varnish or diluted rubber solution.

When the varnish has dried, place the negative in the reducer. The latter will then only affect those parts which have not been covered. After rinsing and drying the negative, the varnish will easily wash off with petrol.

Unsharp Outlines

A negative reduced by the method just described will show a sharp outline between the varnished parts and the reduced area. This may, however, not be desirable, especially if the negative itself is not absolutely sharp.

To achieve a soft outline, apply the reducer by brush and without the help of any resist varnish. Instead of exactly following the outline, the brush should occasionally pass beyond it.

Immediately afterwards, draw a second brush, dipped in plain water, along the outline several times so as to soften it slightly.

SHARP OUTLINES

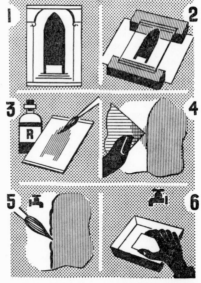

1. To reduce a sharply defined area such as an over-exposed window in an interior view proceed as follows (p. 59).

2. Support the negative face up across two books or boxes above a sheet of white paper.

3. Carefully apply the reducer with a brush.

4. If the brush passes over the line immediately mop up the surplus solution with blotting paper, and

5. follow this by washing over with water from a second clean brush.

6. Finally wash the whole negative thoroughly.

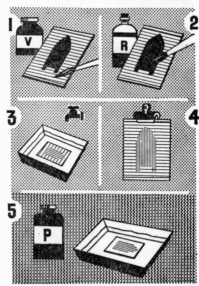

1. An alternative method consists of applying a coat of varnish over the whole of the negative except the area to be treated (p. 60).

2. Paint the reducer over the uncovered area. Alternatively the whole plate can be immersed in the reducer.

3. After sufficient reduction, wash the negative well, and

4. hang up to dry.

5. Finally remove the resist varnish with a suitable solvent (e.g., petrol).

Another method of obtaining a soft outline is to apply the reducer to a wet plate or film. The negative must in that case lie absolutely flat.

Alternatively, instead of wetting the negative before reduction, it can be soaked in sodium thiosulphate solution and then treated with potassium ferricyanide reducer. If mixed with a good proportion of glycerine, the reducer becomes viscous and easier to handle.

The following procedure gives reliable results. Prepare a 50 per cent solution of sodium thiosulphate and dilute it with an equal volume of glycerine. Soak the negative in this for several minutes, then remove and allow surplus liquid to drain off. As the glycerine retains the moisture, there is no danger of the negative drying prematurely during treatment.

Then apply ferricyanide reducer with a brush to the parts to be treated.

3.—POTASSIUM FERRICYANIDE REDUCER

Potassium ferricyanide	1 ounce	25 grams
Water	4 ounces	100 c.cm.
Glycerine	½ ounce	12 c.cm.

This solution acts very evenly. In order to observe the progress, stop the action of the reducer from time to time by returning the plate to the sodium thiosulphate bath. Before doing so, remove excess reducer by inclining the plate and holding the lower corners against a piece of blotting paper.

Each time the negative is removed from the fixer it must be carefully placed in a rack to drain.

Finally, give the negative a thorough rinse.

Intensification

Just as dense parts of a negative can be made lighter by reduction, so thinner areas can be intensified. The various operations are similar to those already described.

Thus the intensifier can be poured over larger areas or

SOFT OUTLINES

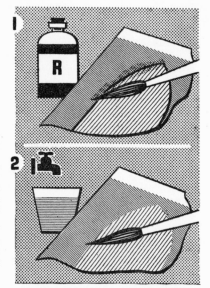

Reduction with the help of a resist mask sometimes leaves excessively sharp outlines which may be undesirable if the negative is not perfectly sharp.

1. To soften the outline apply very dilute reducer along it. Do not follow the outline exactly but go a little to either side of it (p. 60).

2. Immediately follow this with a second brush charged with water to soften the outline. Repeat this several times.

INTENSIFICATION

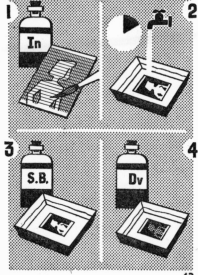

Local intensification can be carried out similarly to local reduction though the solutions are different. With a copper intensifier the procedure is exactly the same as with the reducer; the chromium intensifier needs several stages as follows (p. 64).

1. Brush the intensifier solution (which is a bleaching bath) over the area to be treated.

2. When bleached, thoroughly wash the negative for at least ten minutes in running water.

3. Rinse in a stop bath of potassium metabisulphite to remove all stain.

4. Redevelop the image in a normal developer.

applied with a brush, or those parts not intended for treatment can first be covered with a resist varnish and the negative then placed in an intensifier bath. Two intensifiers suitable for handling in this manner are copper and chromium.

4.—COPPER INTENSIFIER

Potassium citrate, 10% solution	2¼ ounces	60 c.cm.
Copper sulphate, 10% solution	160 minims	8 c.cm.
Potassium ferricyanide, 10% solution	140 minims	7 c.cm.

5.—CHROMIUM INTENSIFIER

Potassium Bichromate, 5% solution	2 parts
Hydrochloric Acid, 5% solution	1 part
Water	1 part

Copper intensification has the advantage of being a one-solution process, but the copper tones the area affected red. Some experience is required to judge the correct degree of intensification.

Chromium intensification takes place in two separate operations. First bleach the image by painting the intensifier solution over the required portions. After bleaching, rinse in running water for about 10 minutes followed by a 5 per cent potassium metabisulphite bath and finally darken the negative in a normal developer (*not* a fine grain formula).

The various reducers and intensifiers are also available in commercially packed form.

THE DESK

Most negative retouching methods to be described below require a special retouching desk.

The retouching desk is to the photographer what the easel is to the painter. It consists essentially of an inclined frame containing a ground glass screen on which we lay the negative for treatment by brush, pencil or knife.

Retouching by Daylight

Correct placing of the desk is important.

The negative is viewed and all treatment carried out by transmitted light. The back of the desk should therefore face a window so that the daylight shines through the negative from behind. Any light shining on the negative from the front will affect the clarity of vision.

Some types of desk have an additional upper frame fastened at right angles to the negative stage, and covered with black cloth to cut off side and top light. If the cloth is large enough it will also serve to cut off light shining on to the negative from the front.

We look down through the ground glass towards the table. A mirror on the table reflects the daylight up to the ground glass. The mirror should be carefully adjusted so as to illuminate the whole of the ground glass.

For more diffused lighting, a sheet of white card may be used instead of the mirror.

Retouching by Artificial light

A mirror is less suitable for use with electric bulbs and should be replaced or covered over with a piece of smooth

R.—C

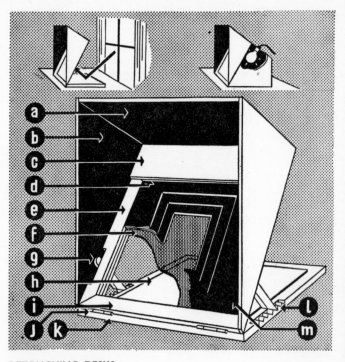

RETOUCHING DESKS

A retouching desk is essential for many negative retouching methods. It supports the negative and also illuminates it from behind.

Top left : The retouching desk consists of an inclined easel which carries the negative. A sheet of white paper or mirror underneath reflects the light from the window or other light source through the negative. A hood round the top of the easel prevents all outside light from falling on the negative.

Top right : To make the desk independent of all prevailing light, an electric light bulb can be built into the desk behind the easel itself.

You can construct a useful retouching desk at home from a few suitable pieces of wood. No measurements are given since they depend largely on the sizes of the negatives to be treated.

The frame of the easel consists of two side pieces (e) joined to a bottom (i) and a top member (d). A panel (c) keeps the top together. The parts of the frame (d), (e) and (i) are recessed on the inside to take a sheet of flashed opal glass (f) which acts as a diffuser. For additional strength, a pair of angle plates (n) can be screwed to the bottom of the **frame.**

66

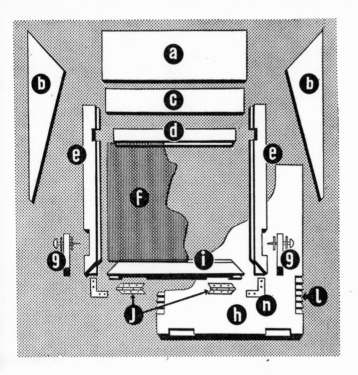

A hood consisting of the top *a* and two side pieces *b* can be nailed or screwed to the frame.

The frame itself is hinged to the base board (*k*) with two hinges (*j*). A sheet of white paper (*h*) on the baseboard serves as a reflector.

Two movable struts (*g*) screwed into the recessed sides (*e*) of the frame engage in the rack (*l*) cut into the sides of the baseboard. This permits the desk to be adjusted to any angle for convenient working.

A set of masks (*m*) for different negative sizes fits over the opal glass and cuts down the illuminated area to the actual size of the negative. This facilitates retouching as it eliminates disturbing outside light.

To finish the job, paint the inside of the hood as well as the frame itself black. A small movable mask with a circular cut-out will restrict the light even further to the actual working area of any negative (p. 84).

white card. The small area of the light source would provide uneven illumination if reflected in a mirror, and some means of diffusion is therefore required.

Many retouching desks are designed as a light box, incorporating its own light source. This is a more compact arrangement, but may warm up the negative too much for dye retouching (the dyes dry up too quickly). Retouching boxes therefore need adequate ventilation.

Some people may find retouching by the yellowish light of ordinary electric bulbs a strain. In that case it is best to use daylight bulbs or fluorescent strip lighting.

A liquid filter can also modify half-watt or tungsten lamp light to give it daylight quality. It consists of a dilute solution of ammoniacal copper sulphate in a glass trough (e.g., a narrow aquarium) and is placed between the lamp and the cardboard reflector.

6.—LIQUID FILTER

Copper Sulphate	I part
Water	1,000–2,000 parts

The concentration required will depend on the thickness of the liquid filter ; the thicker the solution layer, the more dilute it should be.

Add dilute ammonia to the above solution. A pale blue precipitate first forms ; add more ammonia until this precipitate completely dissolves in a clear blue solution.

The Ground Glass

The ground glass must be placed in its frame with the matt surface facing away from the negative.

This has two reasons. The smooth glass surface is easier to keep clean ; and there is no danger of injuring films laid against it for treatment. If pressed against the matt side of the glass, films may get scratched, and the effect is as if they had been rubbed with a sheet of fine sandpaper. There is, however, no danger of scratching plates.

If the grain of the screen is disturbing, use a flashed opal glass sheet instead.

Some retouching desks carry a nest of interchangeable ground-glass screens ; it is then an easy matter to use one of the right size for the negative to be retouched.

Further refinements are a rotating negative stage, and a magnifying glass on an adjustable arm.

Correct Posture

Place the retouching desk on a substantial table, at least a foot deeper than the desk itself.

As painting and drawing are often done on a horizontal surface, working on an inclined desk may seem a little strange at first. If the desk is placed a few inches from the edge of the table, this will provide room to rest the elbows and give some support.

Do not bend down over the desk and peer into the negative. Sit up fairly straight with the head some distance from the inclined surface of the desk.

Make sure that the desk stands firmly on the table. If it slips away during retouching operations, damage to the negative may result.

DYE AND PIGMENT RETOUCHING

Holding Back

Many negatives, though adequately exposed in the highlights, have relatively weak shadows which block up at once when printed and lose all detail. The harder the grade of paper used, the more obvious the defect becomes. An application of suitable dye to the shadows will serve to hold them back when printed and retain the detail.

Holding back should not be confused with local intensification.

The former is employed when the parts requiring treatment have sufficient shadow detail, but the highlights are so dense that the long exposure required to print them results in loss of all shadow details. A red dye, applied to the shadow areas of the negative, restrains the action of the light and prevents blocking up.

Local intensification is only employed on parts of negatives where detail is insufficient.

Another method of reducing excessive contrast between highlights and shadow areas of a negative is to reduce the highlights (p. 58). It is, therfore, a question of either treating shadows or highlights ; and it is best to choose the method involving treatment of the smallest area.

Equipment

The necessary equipment consists of two soft brushes—preferably on the large scale—and a suitable red dye like neo-coccine which has the property of colouring the gelatine layer and remaining fast in it. The red dye of a set of photo-tints is often equally suitable.

It is best to make up two solutions, one more dilute

HOLDING BACK

Areas of negatives that print too dark can be held back by applying red or black negative dye diluted (p. 70).

1. Apply the diluted dye evenly over the area.

2. The dye may tend to collect in corners of the image outline and leave a blob ; when lifting the brush draw it away from the corner.

3. Repeated applications of the diluted dye are better than one application of strong solution. You do not need to follow the outlines exactly. This blends the held back area more evenly with its surroundings.

On plate negatives the dye must be applied on the emulsion side (*left*). On roll film negatives which have a gelatine backing, the dye may be painted over that.

A resist varnish is useful to protect small areas while applying the dye.

1. Paint the areas which do not require treatment with the varnish.

2. Apply the dye or immerse the negative in a dilute solution of it.

3. When the area is sufficiently tinted, dry the negative and remove the varnish with petrol or other suitable solvent (p. 73).

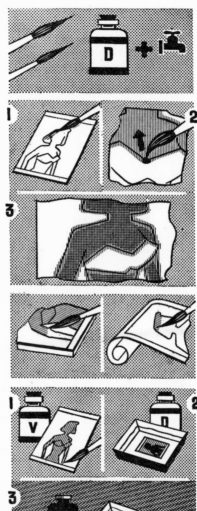

than the other and keep them in stoppered bottles. The weaker solution should be so dilute that if brushed across a sheet of white paper there is only a slight tinge of red in it. The stronger should show plenty of colour, though not as much as, for example, red ink.

Applying the Dye

The whole art of holding back depends on absolutely even application of the dye to the emulsion surface. The more dilute the solutions used, the smaller the risk of spots forming.

Always begin by applying the weaker solution with the large brush. The brush should hold enough dye to form a point. Keep the brush well charged. It will require frequent refilling, as the gelatine coating is very absorbent. On the other hand, it should not be so full that drops of dye fall off it and flow down the negative.

Apply the dye with brisk strokes of the brush to the part of the negative to be treated, carefully following the outline. Be sure to paint over the whole surface as quickly as possible.

Do not work slowly over one part or allow a drop of dye to remain anywhere for any length of time. The inevitable result of doing so would be a dense patch on the negative where the surface has absorbed excess dye.

After a short time all liquid will be drawn out of the brush. When lifting it from the negative surface for replenishment, be sure that the small dot or point of dye that forms as the brush leaves the negative, is directed towards the area under treatment. It should on no account face towards the edge, as this would form a noticeable blob of dye (p. 86).

In order to blend the area treated into its surroundings, do not follow the outlines exactly at every application of dye. Go over the edges a little with one wash of dye and keep slightly inside with the next one.

Keep the brush well charged with dye solution all the time. When wet, the hairs are harmless to the emulsion

72

layer ; but dry hairs are apt to cause tiny scratches on the swollen gelatine.

Judging the Effect

The effect of the dye builds up with successive applications. The more washes we paint over the required area, the more intense the colouring becomes and the lighter it will print. If a really strong colour is required, use the concentrated solution for the final treatment.

Estimating the right density needs a certain amount of experience, as it is not always easy to gauge visually the printing effect of a coloured dye. Beginners usually apply too much dye. One way of assessing the effect is to look at the image through half-closed eyes. The red then seems to blend into the grey image, showing the apparent density.

Another method is to view the work through a green or blue filter, when the colours will be seen as shades of grey.

As an alternative to red dye, grey negative dyes are marketed by several firms. Negatives retouched with grey dye show the effect much more plainly. Red dyes like neococcine and retouching red can, however, be completely removed by rinsing ; the grey dyes sometimes leave a tinge.

With plates, all holding back with dye must be carried out on the film side. Roll and flat films may be treated on the back, as this also has a gelatine covering ; but it is sometimes hardened and will only absorb a small amount of dye. On the other hand the hardening renders the surface less liable to be scratched by dry hairs of the brush.

Matt film backing is not a suitable surface for dyes.

Dyeing by Immersion

Even with a large brush it is difficult to apply dye evenly to large areas of a negative such as the sky. In such cases it is advisable to follow the procedure already recommended for local reduction (p. 60). Simply varnish those parts which are not to be treated, then place the negative in a bath of dye solution.

Films (except miniature films) must be varnished on the back as well, otherwise the dye will soak in there too.

The varnish is removed with petrol or turpentine after drying the negative.

Spotting

There is one form of negative treatment which no photographer can avoid, even if he does not believe in re-touching ; and that is spotting. It sometimes happens, even when the greatest care is exercised, that particles of dust or film emulsion adhere to the sensitive layer, causing unexposed pinholes which appear black in the print.

In addition, certain bacteria can get on to the negative during washing or drying and literally eat away small spots of gelatine down to the film or glass base.

There are two reasons why it is better to remove these spots from the negative than from the print. In the first place, spotting the negative saves all work on the print : we have to do the job only once instead of every time we make a print. Secondly, black spots have to be removed from a print with a knife. This damages the surface and usually leaves a dull mark.

Dye and Pigment Media

There are two kinds of spotting media—dye, and pigment.

The former is a solution which dyes the gelatine and is difficult to wash out. It is, in fact, the same as the grey negative dye used for holding back (p. 73). When applied, the dye itself sinks into the gelatine, and leaves no trace on the surface. As it is transparent, it blends well with the image and does not become conspicuous even at high degrees of enlargement. But it can be used only where there is a gelatine layer it can dye. By itself the dye has practically no covering power.

Make	Dye	Pigment	Opaque
Agfa	Neucoccin		
Craftint			Negative opaque Cel-flex
Gilby	Plumtree neutral grey retouching dye		Plumtree liquid opaque Plumtree Plastor opaque
Grey-Al. Co.	Grey-Al. Dye		
Höchst (Pina)	Photo tints (black, blue-black, brown, deep brown, chocolate, neutral grey)		
Halie		Glossy retouching colours (white, vermilion, red, indigo) Matt retouching colours (vermilion, red, indigo)	Black and red-brown opaque
Johnsons	Negative dye	Spotting medium	Liquid opaque
Klimsch		Black negative colour	
Kodak	Spotting black Spotting sepia	Opaque and spotting medium	Opaque
Marabu		Glossy retouching colours (black 106, brown black 114, red brown 112) Matt retouching colours (5 shades of grey 101, black 109, brown black 115, red brown 113) Airbrush white 106 R, 107 R	Black opaque 111 Red-brown opaque 110 Vermilion
Pelikan (Günther Wagner)	Pelikan tints type 54 (black, indigo, sepia, vandyke brown)	Pelikan lamp black 23 Pelikan airbrush white 49 and 51 ; airbrush black airbrush brown Pelikan positive retouching	Red opaque

Make	Dye	Pigment	Opaque
Pelikan (cont.)		colours type 49 (matt), type 51 (glossy) (sepia ; pale, light, and med. grey, brown red, blue-black, black)	
Philadelphus Jeyes	Martin's retouching dyes (black, brown, grey)		
Patents Parent Corporation	PPC Neutral grey retouching dye PPC Red retouching dye		
Schmincke	Photo-red 62	Airbrush white A and DD Glossy and matt retouching colours (blue-black, black, brown black)	Opaque 61 black Opaque 1460
Vanguard			Photopaque
Winsor & Newton		W. & N. glossy retouching colours (black, blue-black, sepia, red-brown) W. & N. spotting and retouching colours (bromide black, neutral black, photo-black, cool dark brown, warm middle brown, warm light brown, buff brown) W. & N. Photo-engravers' colours (black, white, 5 shades of grey)	W. & N. Photographic opaque

DYE SPOTTING

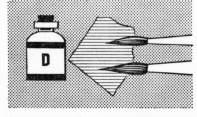

For spotting with dyes we need one or two fine brushes, blotting paper and a grey spotting dye.

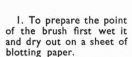

1. To prepare the point of the brush first wet it and dry out on a sheet of blotting paper.

2. Examine the point for straggling hairs.

3. Singe off these by passing the tip of the brush quickly through a flame to form

4. a perfect point (p. 78).

To spot pinholes proceed as follows :

1. Dilute the dye to the required tint.

2. Draw the charged brush across the blotting paper to form a point and also test the tint.

3. Paint the spot out with the brush until

4. it matches the surroundings in density.

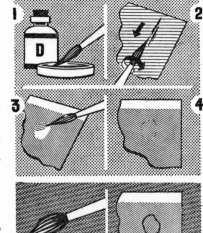

Do not fill the brush too full or the dye will form a circular ring round the spot treated.

Water colour pigment, opaque, and other pigment media are not solutions but suspensions of finely powdered pigment. They are body colours and form a layer of pigment on the surface. Combined with a suitable binding medium they can be applied anywhere, even on clear film or glass. At high degrees of enlargement they show the granular structure of the individual pigment grains. They have great covering power, and are therefore more suitable for complete blocking out. The surface film so formed is easily washed off.

Most of the spotting media supplied are pigments. One way to tell is to see whether the instructions say anything about shaking the bottle before use. Dye solutions are homogeneous, but pigment media have to be shaken up to mix them thoroughly.

There is a difference between spots caused by dust, where the gelatine underneath is intact, and spots which are actual holes in the gelatine layer.

The former can be removed by careful spotting with a negative dye ; the latter need filling in with water colour or pigment spotting medium.

The Brush

A small brush with a very fine point is required. Most brushes form a point with one or two specially long protruding hairs. For our purposes the point should consist of several hairs which will support one another so that single hairs do not break away and form a row of dots or thin secondary lines.

The best method of dealing with straggling hairs is singeing. First dip the point in water then, while rotating the handle, form a sharp point by drawing the hairs across a sheet of blotting paper. Next strike a match and hold the hairs for a brief moment in the flame. This will burn off all protruding hairs.

PIGMENT SPOTTING

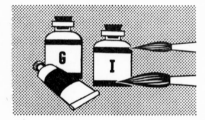

The materials for pigment spotting are Indian ink, gum and water colour together with one or two brushes.

Indian ink is useful for treating small spots in dense areas where a single application will fill in the spot (p. 80).

For larger areas make up a suitable strength of water colour and stipple in the area with a brush (p. 105).

Scratches and similar flaws in glass negatives which leave clear holes must be treated differently (p. 105).

1. Mix up the water colour medium with a little gum to form a thin smooth paste.

2. This is necessary because neither dye nor pigments will take easily on glass but would only colour the gelatine.

3. Fill in the spot with the gum medium.

4. It is usually difficult to match densities exactly so fill in the spot darker than required ; it can then be rectified on the print.

Spotting with Dye

Spotting methods vary according to whether the gelatine layer is still intact at the point affected, or is damaged leaving clear glass or film exposed.

If the gelatine layer is intact, spotting is effected with dye.

Dyes have the property of colouring the gelatine, and once absorbed they remain fast.

Repeated applications of the dye will progressively darken the spot until the density of the surroundings is matched.

Dip the brush in the dye and draw it across a blotter while twisting to form a point. The brush should be as dry as possible, so that the dye applied is lighter in shade than the image area under treatment. Never fill the brush so full that the dye flows out of it and on to the negative, as it will inevitably form a circular mark round the point to be retouched.

Treat larger spots first with dilute grey, passing the brush across them repeatedly until the surrounding tone is matched.

The beginner may have difficulty in getting the right density. In such a case it is best to err on the dark rather than on the light side. If all efforts at matching fail, it is best to block out the spot completely. This will leave a corresponding white spot on the print which can easily be removed.

Spotting with Pigment

If a light-coloured spot is surrounded by a much denser area, use Indian ink or water colour instead of transparent dye. To prepare the water colour, rub the brush on the pill of colour, then apply to the negative in a single gentle dab with the tip of the brush. The correct density must in this case be reached in one application, for the water colour is not a dye and therefore does not colour the gelatine. Repeated application would only cause a smear.

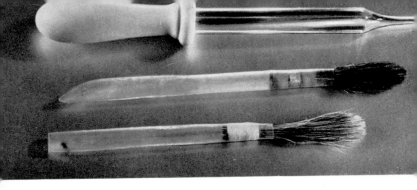

On page 81: WET RETOUCHING. Chemical retouching involves treatment of parts of the negative with reducers (p. 58) or intensifiers (p. 62). The simplest case is that of a dense sky (p. 81, *top*) which will not print through sufficiently to show detail of the clouds. Therefore, the sky has to be reduced. As the horizon is a straight line, the easiest method is to paint the foreground over with a waterproof resist (p. 60), and then insert the whole negative in Farmer's reducer (p. 58). The resist is washed off after treatment is complete. The resulting straight print (p. 81, *bottom*) shows not only the clouds, but also the ship on the horizon which was hidden by the glare of the sky.

LOCAL REDUCTION. Smaller negative areas can also be reduced with the help of a dropping tube and one or two small brushes in quill handles (*above*).

Where parts near the edge of the plate are involved, we can flow the reducer on to the image from a piece of cotton wool (*opposite, top left*). The negative is held over a dish containing the solution to catch the reducer as it flows off (p. 58).

To treat an area near the middle (*opposite, top right*) drop the reducer on it from a dropping tube. Rinse well from time to time. When working with film negatives, clip or tape them to a clean glass plate to hold them flat.

An alternative method is to lay the plate down flat between two boxes or a similar support, and paint the solution over the area required (*opposite, bottom left*). A little glycerine added to the reducer makes it more viscous to simplify handling. A white reflector below the negative permits easy observation of the image.

Where very dense areas are involved, put the negative into the bottom of a glass dish (*opposite, bottom right*) while painting on the reducer. Hold the dish over a lamp to follow the action of the reducer on the image.

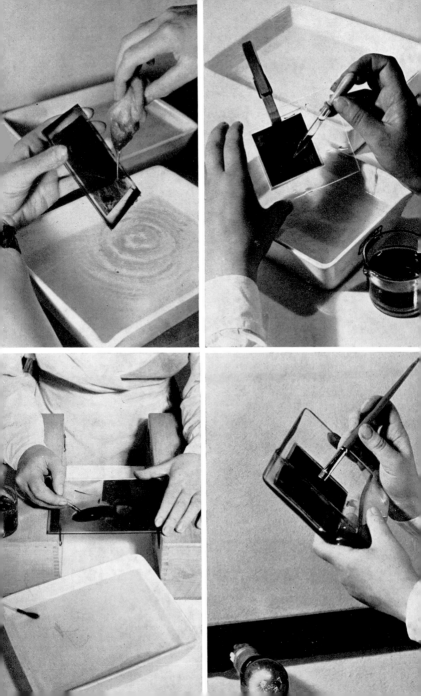

THE RETOUCHING DESK. For working by daylight, the desk is set up in front of a window so that the light is reflected through the negative by a mirror behind (*opposite, top left*). A board at the top and sides screens off disturbing side light (see also p. 66). With artificial light a white paper reflector is preferable for more diffused light (*opposite, bottom left*). A liquid filter may be used to obtain light of approximately daylight quality (p. 68). A magnifying glass (*opposite, top right*) makes for easier working. Another refinement is the retouching box (*opposite, bottom right*), a wooden box with built-in lamp which illuminates a sheet of opal glass.

POSTURE. When working at the desk, sit up straight and relaxed (*above right*). Poring hunched up over the work in a cramped position (*above left*) is tiring.

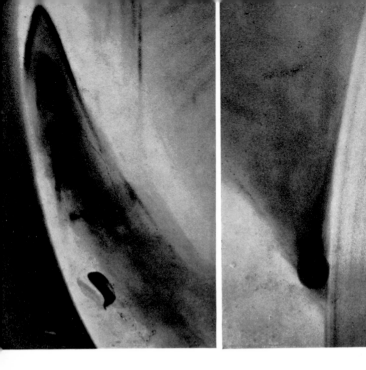

HOLDING BACK. The secret of successful treatment of negatives with dye (p. 70) is to work with dilute solutions. Uneven application of too strong dye shows up as streaks at great magnifications (*above left*).

At sharp corners of the image to be held back, paint out of the corner rather than into it. Otherwise the last drop of dye solution remains as a blob of greater density, especially if the brush is charged too full (*above right*).

Whole negative areas can be treated with dye, for instance when a fussy background is to be suppressed (*opposite top*). In such a case apply a resist layer to the negative with a brush, carefully following the outline of the image, and then immerse the whole in a dilute dye bath (p. 73) to give the emulsion a very weak tinge. That helps to lift the figures out of their surroundings which thus print lighter (*opposite, bottom*).

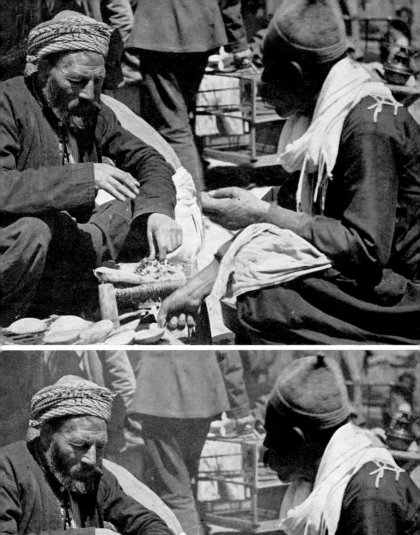

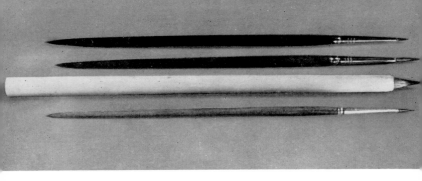

SPOTTING. For taking out small clear spots (p. 74) get a range of camelhair or sable brushes (*above*). Burn off stray hairs with a match (p. 78) to obtain a perfect point (*below left*), otherwise the brush will never produce a round spot (*below right*).

To treat a spot due to an air bell in development (*opposite, top left*) dab it with a fairly dry brush holding colour of the right strength (*opposite, top right*). Too wet a brush produces blobs with a dark rim (*opposite, bottom left*). With difficult spots it may be better to block out altogether (*opposite, bottom right*) and then spot on the print.

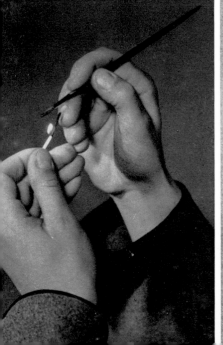

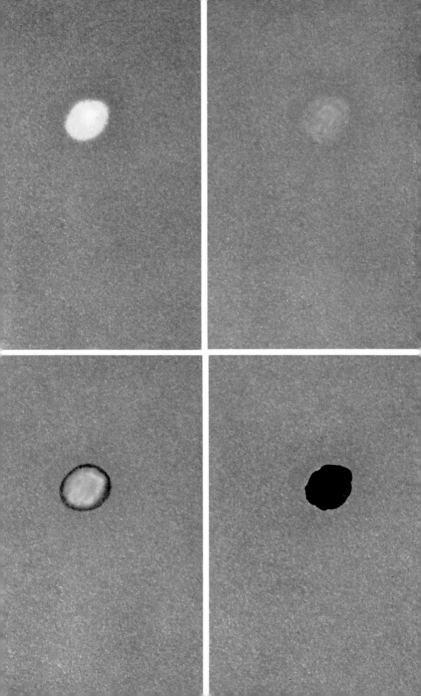

DYE RETOUCHING.
Dye applied with a fine
brush can also be used for
retouching of fine detail on
the negative. When work-
ing, support the hand on a
piece of blotting paper.
Use the magnifier (*right*)
to observe the area under
treatment.

Avoid light falling on the
negative from the front
(*above left*), the image
should be lit only from
behind (*above right*).

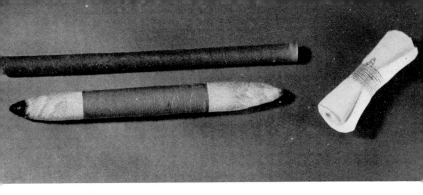

ABRASIVE RETOUCHING, the tools (*above*) are a glass fibre brush, a pointed paper stump and a felt stump for large areas.

When working with a paste (*below left*) moisten the stump first in the medium (p. 110) and then in the abrasive powder. Powder alone (*below right*) is safer but slower. Work over the area continuously until sufficiently reduced.

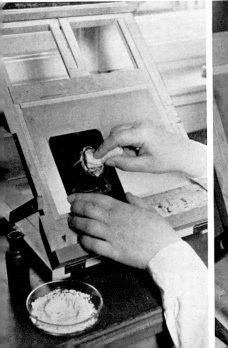

DRY REDUCTION. Applied with a pointed stump, a dry reducer can be used to lighten even comparatively small areas, such as over-brilliant rim lighting in a portrait (*above*), or flare spots and halation around bright light sources in outdoor shots at night (*opposite, top*). To deal with the flare spot, the circle may first be rubbed with a pointed match-stick carrying the abrasive, and the lighter area within the circle reduced with a small stump (*opposite, bottom*). See also p. 91.

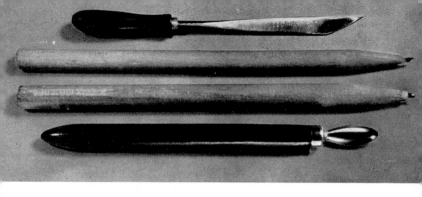

KNIFING. A knife with a long blade (*above*) is most suitable for scraping large areas, while the shorter blades, straight and rounded, are for smaller spots. The edges need frequent sharpening (*below left*) and honing (*below right*). See also p. 111.

To scrape an area work in close, parallel strokes, then go over the area a second time, with the strokes at an angle to the first lot (*opposite top*).

If the blade is too thin, it will vibrate and scratch rather than scrape (*opposite, bottom left*) giving an uneven result. Another fault is to cut too deep; that easily cuts away through the emulsion layer to the base (*opposite, bottom right*).

RETOUCHING PENCILS. Pencils should have a long, sharp point. A short point (*above, bottom*) does not permit fine enough strokes.

To sharpen the pencil, rub it to and fro on a piece of sandpaper, holding the lead almost flat on the paper and rotating it while rubbing (*below*).

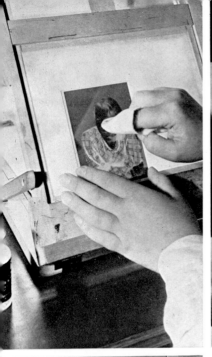

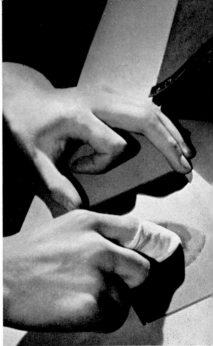

PREPARING THE NEGATIVE. Rub a little retouching medium or matt varnish (p. 120) over the surface of the negative (*above*). Cover the whole surface evenly, otherwise patches may show up during printing.

Alternatively, the negative may be covered by a sheet of matt film which has the advantage that it can be stripped off at any time (*left*).

HOLDING THE PENCIL. The correct way to hold the pencil is well back from the point (*above left*) in a light grip. This permits maximum control of the lead, without the danger of the point breaking off through excessive pressure.

When held too short (*above right*), the fine control is missing as the pressure is too great. This applies excessive density in one lot, instead of building it up gradually.

PENCIL RETOUCHING. The most straightforward job to start on is the correction of eye shadows on a portrait (*left*). The correct grade of pencil is important ; too hard a lead, especially on top of too thick a layer of re-touching medium (p. 126), pushes the coating of medium aside and causes smears and smudges (*below left*). Even pencilling with the right lead should blend in almost invisibly (*below right*).

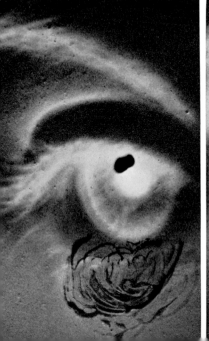

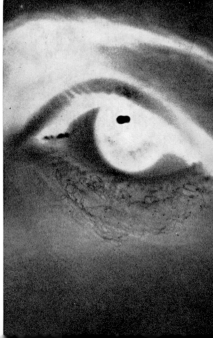

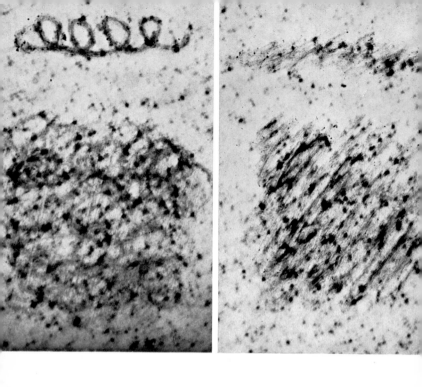

PENCIL STROKES. There are two ways of building up density, by drawing spirals (*left*) or short, straight lines (*right*). When highly magnified, the spirals appear to blend in better with the grain structure of the image, as the individual lines disappear when superimposed several times. Straight lines, however, tend to show up even when combined in a comparatively larger area (p. 127).

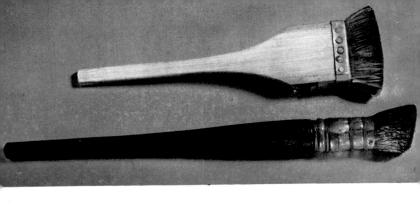

RETOUCHING ON THE BACK OF THE NEGATIVE. Mostly this consists of the application of pigment to the glass side, by means of suitable dabbing brushes (*above*). The colour is dabbed on over the area to be controlled (*below right*), and the outline of the image then washed out with an ordinary fine brush. Small areas can be treated with graphite powder (*below left*) applied to the varnished back by a stump (p. 129).

BLOCKING OUT. To produce a completely blank background on the print, the negative may be blocked out on the emulsion side with black dye and opaque pigment (p. 132). The first step is to paint a border around the image with black dye, softening the outline by washing it out with a brush charged with water (*left*). The rest of the background can then be covered up with opaque pigment (*right*) up to the dye border.

The opaque should not go beyond the outer edge of the dye border, as it would otherwise destroy the soft outline. Also, mistakes are often only noticed when the job is finished. Correcting the dye outline would then soil the brush with opaque, and make a mess of things.

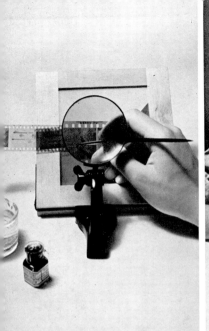

RETOUCHING MINIATURE NEGATIVES. The smallness of the detail to be handled makes a magnifier indispensable. With care, an appreciable amount of spotting and minor correction is possible even on 35 mm. film (p. 140).

When working support the hand on a piece of card, backed by leather, which presses the film against the glass, and protects the emulsion from fingerprints (*left*).

Magnifying spectacles (*right*) makes the job still more comfortable. However, as this entails working very close to the desk, keep a folded piece of paper between the lips to avoid breathing directly on the negative.

CRACKED PLATES. When a glass plate has got broken but the emulsion layer is still in one piece, it is best to make a duplicate by contact printing (p. 138).

The plate is placed into a printing frame, and the crack filled in from the face side of the frame with oil diluted with petrol (*left*). The latter helps the oil to fill the crack, and should have evaporated before printing. During the exposure, rotating the frame above the light source prevents the crack from casting shadows (*right*).

Actual holes in the gelatine resulting from mechanical damage to the emulsion layer require different treatment. Dye is again useless as there is no vehicle to absorb it. Indian ink is also unsuitable as it would darken the spot excessively.

In such cases, water colour is the best medium, and may be diluted according to the shade required, using a fairly dry brush. Mix the colour with a little gum to prevent it flaking off the film or glass base when dry.

In the case of large areas, the colour must be stippled on by applying a series of dots one beside the other. After any area has been once treated do not attempt to brush it over a second time ; this will inevitably leave a smear.

These methods will not render the spot entirely invisible ; but fortunately negatives are seldom so badly damaged that whole pieces of emulsion are missing.

ABRASIVE RETOUCHING

Parts of a negative that are too dense can be reduced either chemically (p. 56) or mechanically. In the former case the dense areas are lightened by dissolving part of the silver deposit ; in mechanical or dry reduction the same result is obtained by rubbing down or abrading the top layer of the emulsion.

It is impossible to lay down a hard and fast rule as to when dry reduction is preferable to chemical treatment. In general it is more suitable for dealing with smaller areas.

If a whole negative is to be reduced, dry reduction would hardly be appropriate, as chemical treatment is both simpler and more uniform in action.

A special case of abrasive retouching is knifing ; there we remove very small details by scraping them down.

Stumps

The grinding medium should be as fine as possible so as not to affect the enlarging properties of the negative. The most practical method of applying the abrasive powder to the negative is an artist's stump. These are available in different sizes to suit the area to be treated. Stumps are made of leather or paper ; paper is to be preferred, and is in any case cheaper. Paper stumps can be made out of strips of fibrous paper tightly rolled and sharpened at one end with sand-paper.

For large areas a felt stump is useful, rolled in the same way as paper, but left blunt at the end.

Small cotton-wool pads tightly wrapped in linen, or leather can also be used in place of stumps.

ABRASIVE MEDIA

For dry reduction we can use abrasive powders and media. The tools are large and small stumps for treating areas of different sizes (p. 106).

The powder used in abrasive pastes can be either Kieselguhr or pumice. In either case it should be washed to get the powder really fine (p. 110).

1. Stir the finely sifted powder into a large beaker or tumbler of water.

2. Leave to stand for a time to allow the coarser grains to settle.

3. Decant the liquid carrying the finer grains in suspension.

4. Discard the coarse residue.

5. Filter the suspension through filter paper.

6. Dry the powder on the paper.

If the area to be reduced is very small, it can be treated with a small piece of wood with the end sharpened to a point or shaped like a chisel.

Abrasive Powders and Pastes

The reducing medium may be used dry or in semi-liquid form, but should contain no water, as the gelatine must be kept quite dry throughout the reducing process. The smallest water content would swell the gelatine and damage to the emulsion layer would be inevitable.

The most reliable media are pumice powder and old-fashioned plate powder formerly used for cleaning silver. Plate powder is seldom available nowadays, as more effective preparations for silver-cleaning have replaced it ; but the latter are of no use for our purpose, as they contain water. We give below formulae for preparing two dry reducers. The abrasive pastes can also be prepared at home.

7.—DRY REDUCER

Paraffin Wax	2 ounces	50 grams
Tallow	3 ounces	75 grams
Vaseline	8 ounces	200 grams
Oleic Acid	5 ounces	125 grams
Nitrobenzene	20 minims	2 c.cm.

Melt the mixture to form a smooth paste, and while still warm, stir in:

Tripoli (finest Kieselguhr)	20 ounces	500 grams

Pour the paste into a tin to cool.

8.—ALTERNATIVE DRY REDUCER

Ceresin	1¼ ounces	30 grams
Oleine	5 ounces	120 grams
Vaseline	8 ounces	200 grams

Melt as before, and stir in :

Tripoli (finest Kieselguhr)	20 ounces	500 grams

The finer the Tripoli is in both cases, the smoother the resulting paste. To obtain a specially smooth mixture, sift or wash the Tripoli beforehand.

Pumice powder is an alternative medium ; it has to be washed to get it really fine.

DRY REDUCTION

Dry reducers are used as follows (p. 110).

1. Dip the stump in the medium (a turpentine mixture).

2. Dip the soaked stump in the powder.

Alternatively apply the reducing paste to the stump directly.

3. Rub the stump over the surface to be treated until area is sufficiently reduced.

4. Wipe the negative with a piece of cotton wool to remove all the powder and clean the surface.

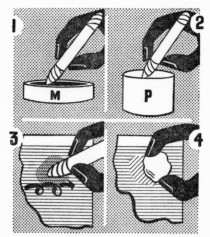

As soon as the end of the stump appears soiled, clean it by rubbing on a piece of fine sand paper.

To obtain sharp outlines by dry reduction (p. 111).

1. Trace the outline of the area to be treated on a sheet of thin celluloid.

2. Cut out the mask.

3. Position it over the negative.

4. Apply the dry reducer, working it well over the edges of the mask.

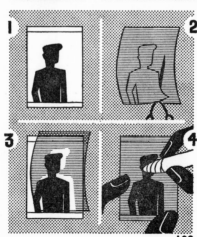

This is done by pouring the finely sifted powder (pumice or Tripoli) into a fair-sized vessel of water, while stirring the liquid. Leave the vessel standing for a time, during which the heavier coarser grains sink to the bottom. Carefully decant the liquid in which the finer grains have remained suspended, so that the coarser grains remain behind. The longer the liquid is left standing, the finer the powder will be. Finally filter the water off and dry the powder.

Pumice powder can either be used dry or mixed with the following alternative reducer :

9.—ABRASIVE MEDIUM

Oil of turpentine	l part
Petrol or carbon tetrachloride	l part

Applying the Abrasive

To reduce large areas with pumice powder, soak a cloth in the medium, then dip it in the powder and rub it over the surface with a circular motion until the area in question is sufficiently reduced.

Paraffin wax and ceresin reducers are applied in the same way.

For smaller negative areas use a stump, dipping it first in the liquid, then in the paste.

Do not attempt to economize with powder or paste reducer ; both should be applied liberally as they rapidly lose their abrasiveness with use. Avoid applying strong pressure as this will result in uneven reduction. Dry reducing is slow work and calls for a certain amount of patience.

The pointed ends of paper stumps soon get smeared over with silver deposit and pumice powder and should be frequently cleaned with sand-paper. Make sure that no broken bits of sand-paper remain sticking to the stump afterwards.

Once the desired degree of reduction is reached, the

powder or paste must be removed from the negative surface. First wipe the negative over with a wad of cotton wool ; this will remove most of the reducer. Then take another wad to remove any residue, and polish the surface until it shines.

Sharp outlines are not obtainable by normal methods of dry reduction, a fact which has its advantages and disadvantages. If a sharp outline is required, as sometimes happens, cut a mask out of an old film and place it over the part of the negative which is not to be treated. Use a fairly large stump and work it well over the edges of the mask. The reducer will, of course, only affect those parts of the negative not masked off.

For the sake of completeness we should mention the glass brushes sold for removing inkspots from paper. They can serve very well for dry reduction work as the fine glass hairs are very sharp. The only disadvantage is that negatives will not stand much enlargement after treatment

Knifework

While the abrasive technique described in the preceding chapter is only used to lighten parts of a negative, the retouching knife serves to remove detail altogether. As the knife is only employed when parts of the image are to be entirely eliminated, its uses are strictly limited.

Proper handling of the retouching knife requires considerable skill and practice ; it is in fact the most difficult part of retouching.

The Right Knife

Apart from the skill and practice needed, success in knifework depends on two decisive factors : firstly the choice of knife, and secondly its sharpness.

Essential characteristics of a retouching knife are : a rigid blade of first quality steel, and a cutting edge which is uniformly sharp and shows slight curvature when viewed longitudinally.

Fine work requires a small, narrow blade, larger areas call for a large, broad one.

Knives available on the market are shaped either like a surgical scalpel or artist's spatula. In the hands of a skilled worker the former can be used for most scraping, as both the point and the cutting edge can be used. The spatula type of knife usually has a straight edge and must be reground to a slight curve ; and it is only suitable for treatment of larger areas.

Actual surgical scalpels are often recommended for retouching, but they are not ideal, as the point is often as thin as a razor-blade and liable to vibrate in use. Razor blades and retouching nibs are also unsuitable for the same reason.

Engraving tools as used by process engravers for working on copper plates are specially suitable for very fine work. They consist of long steel cores in a wooden sheath, and can be resharpened like a pencil when the core is worn away.

Sharpening

Correct sharpening of the knife is of first importance and a sharpening stone should be part of the retouching kit. Such stones are available as whetstones and oil-stones. Whetstones are coarser and cut faster. The final honing of the knife should, however, always take place on an oil-stone.

The following is the correct method of sharpening a spatula type knife for use on a larger negative area.

First moisten the stone with a small quantity of oil. Lay the blade on the stone and place the index finger on it so that it extends just up to the cutting edge. Sharpening is more rapid if paraffin is used instead of oil.

Sharpen one side by moving the blade to and fro, taking care to swing the hand from the wrist with a pendulum movement so as to impart a slight curve to the cutting edge. If this is not done a completely straight edge will

KNIFING

Of the various shapes of retouching knives, the thin blades are best for fine work and the wider blades more convenient for large areas.

The knife must be carefully sharpened (p. 112).

1. Apply a few drops of oil on the oil stone, place the blade on it at the appropriate sharpening angle. Keep the blade at the same angle all the time.

2. Move the blade to and fro, and swing it slightly to give the cutting edge a small curvature.

3. Turn the blade over to sharpen the other side.

4. Strop the edge by drawing it across the stone at a higher angle.

Spoon-shaped knives are sharpened by drawing them over the stone with a circular movement.

To reduce the density of a small area, scrape it with parallel strokes set closely to each other (*left*). When the whole area has been scraped, change the direction of the strokes to form a second set at an angle to the first (p. 95).

result. After finishing one side, turn the blade over and sharpen the other side.

Stropping

The final stage of sharpening consists of stropping the blade by drawing it across the stone, cutting edge first, as if intending to cut into the stone itself. For this the knife should be placed at a slightly steeper angle on the stone.

The very last stroke of the knife on the stone should always be made on the side of the blade which faces away from the worker at the retouching desk. As we usually scrape with a downward stroke, it follows that the side of the blade to receive the final stropping on the oil-stone is in most cases that on which the index finger rests when in the working position. If this side is stropped twice or three times, the blade will be even sharper.

To test the blade for sharpness, rest the cutting edge on a finger nail. Instead of sliding off, a really sharp blade will appear to stick to the nail. This test will, however, not indicate whether or not the edge is burred, which must be ascertained by trial under working conditions. If the knife scrapes unevenly, it must be sharpened again. If it is sharp enough, any burr can be removed by stropping it on leather or fine paper in the same way as a barber strops his razor.

Engraving tools, having a double edge, must be sharpened on both sides. When sharpening, swing the knife to and fro so that each edge comes into contact with the stone alternatively. The procedure for stropping is the same, only the edge is placed at a somewhat steeper angle. As the knife is usually drawn from right to left in scraping, the final strokes in stropping should be made in the same direction. If the retoucher works from left to right, movements in the final stropping should follow suit.

Spoon-shaped retouching knives are very useful for treating large areas. Sharpening is simple ; lay the cutting side on the stone and draw it over with a circular movement.

It is important not to press too hard, or a burr will form on the cutting edge.

An oval engraving needle will also make a useful knife. It should be ground to the shape of a chisel by pressing the slanting edge against the stone and drawing it round in a circle. This will produce a sharp oval edge round the surface worked on. When used for retouching this will cut either narrow or broad lines according to the angle at which it is held.

The Correct Stroke

The correct procedure is to make a series of parallel strokes, close to each other. When the whole area has been scraped once, work over it a second time, changing the direction of the strokes so that they run at an angle with those already made. Change the direction again for the third and subsequent treatments. This avoids the formulation of obvious lines on the negative. The more sets of strokes are superimposed the better they will blend.

This is not at all easy at first. The heavy-handed beginner usually removes so much of the emulsion layer with his first strokes that a second application of the knife would cut right through to the film base. That is, of course, quite wrong. The aim should be to scrape a large area so smoothly that the individual strokes are invisible.

Practise on an old negative by taking a dense area about half an inch square and trying to lighten it. Do not aim at extensive reduction, but rather at a slight lightening of the area by scraping a series of lines, one upon the other.

The knife will require frequent resharpening and stropping during the work. This will ultimately make the blade thin and liable to jump or vibrate. The edge will then have to be ground away and a new one cut. The state of the blade can be judged by the musical note emitted during sharpening ; it should emit an even sound. The slightest shudder or squeak is a warning that it may damage the emulsion when least expected.

Removing Spots and Lines

We often have to remove small black spots from a negative. They must on no account be chiselled out, as it were ; treatment is the same as for larger areas, except that the knife strokes must be of almost microscopic fineness. With care, we can eliminate thin black lines satisfactorily by means of a line knife.

The oval-ground engraving scraper already mentioned is particularly suitable for this work.

To ascertain the correct angle for the width of stroke required, first try out the knife on the edge of the plate, then without changing the grip, pass the knife gently and rapidly over the black lines. The same technique is used for removing stray hairs from portraits which show up unpleasantly when lit from behind.

Roughening the Surface

Not all surfaces lend themselves easily to treatment. Plates which have previously been reduced, for instance, are difficult to work on as the knife tends to slip on the polished surface. This difficulty can be overcome by roughening the emulsion layer with the aid of pumice powder.

For roughening purposes, the powder is applied dry. Dip a wad of cotton wool in the powder and rub over the emulsion layer with a circular motion until the shine disappears. If the surface is prepared in this manner the knife will grip easily, and permit smooth and even retouching.

Enlarging Negatives after Knifework

A warning is necessary regarding the enlargement of negatives after scraping. If the enlarger used has a point source of light and a condenser without diffuser, the treated areas may show up strongly ; they may even print white. In this event the remedy is to insert a ground glass, or, better still, a sheet of flashed opal glass between condenser

116

and light source. The scraped area will then print through, though it may need extra exposure.

Alternatively, the negative can be treated with one of the varnishes recommended on p. 120. Carbon tetrachloride can be used as a substitute for varnish. Place a few drops on the emulsion, rub the liquid over the negative and press a sheet of glass down on top to prevent formation of bubbles. There is, however, always a danger of the carbon tetrachloride evaporating during the exposure.

PENCIL RETOUCHING

The retouching pencil is one of the commonest instruments for working on negatives, and its excessive use has brought discredit on the whole technique of retouching.

It once used to be customary to work over portrait negatives until the faces were completely smooth and featureless. Unfortunately portraits are still over-retouched to the point where all individuality is lost.

But what we now consider to be an abuse of retouching, used to be a necessity. Skin blemishes, reproduced by emulsions that were far from orthochromatic, let alone panchromatic, had to be removed if the portrait photographer was to sell his picture. Then, as now, the customer wanted a flattering portrait and tended to prefer an idealized version of him or herself to a good likeness. So even to-day photographers are forced to use the pencil to beautify their sitters, though they no longer work over the whole face.

The many half-tones found in a portrait negative of a human face can be most readily matched by pencil. Its use provides the easiest method of blending and shading.

The Need for Retouching

It is considered good form these days to dismiss pencil retouching with contempt, but we should take a different view. Those who scorn pencil retouching do so only because they do not know how to retouch, thus making a virtue out of a shortcoming. In spite of panchromatic emulsions and special lamps, retouching of portrait negatives cannot be dispensed with.

There are, for instance, many men whose beards, even directly after shaving, leave an ugly, restless shadow on the negative ; it may even sometimes make the sitter look as if he were suffering from some skin disease. Other people have such a blotchy complexion that parts of the unretouched negative look as if air bubbles had formed on the emulsion during development. However characteristic such complexion blemishes may be of the sitter, it will surely be necessary at least to tone them down.

Freckles and Eyeshadows

Freckles are another matter. It may be argued that they are characteristic and should therefore not be removed. Yet some will be denser than others and will need reducing to a uniform level. In fact almost every portrait—except a character portrait—has parts which need retouching if the result is to please the sitter.

Eye shadows are always troublesome : they nearly always print too dark and heavy and this is partly due to the lighting. To eliminate eye shadows, frontal lighting would be required ; but the inevitable result in many poses would be a completely flat rendering of the other features. Consequently lighting is usually arranged to give good modelling of the features, but may produce dark shadows under the eyes.

There would be no sense in altering and upsetting the arrangement of the lamps, already adjusted for best modelling of the features, just to remove the eye shadows. Retouching is often preferable.

Quite apart from the lighting, the skin below the eyes always prints too dark, for the complexion is usually somewhat discoloured there and either brownish or bluish. The difference is so slight that it is not normally noticed, for in real life people are always moving their heads, and so the shadows are broken up by the constant change in the direction of the light. When the features are seen at rest in a portrait, the shadow remains fixed, and we must use the pencil to lighten it.

Psychological Factors

Human vanity is a further factor in favour of pencil retouching. Just as no one likes to admit to being over-weight, so no one relishes seeing a double chin in his or her portrait.

People are accustomed to see themselves in the mirror ; and a woman may be quite unaware that her lips are not shaped like the classical cupid's bow. When she sees her own photograph, it will seem to her to be " the wrong way round," and as every face is unsymmetrical she will see herself, as it were, with new eyes and examine her own features more carefully. She may suddenly find that she does not like the shape of her mouth.

To put it in a nutshell, photographing women calls for a lot of retouching !

Preliminary Varnishing

The first step in pencil retouching is to coat the emulsion surface with a varnish that will take the graphite of the retouching pencil. (Some films for portrait work have a matt back requiring no such treatment.) A resinous coating is spread over the plate and provides a " tooth " to hold the graphite.

The composition of the varnish varies according to whether the treatment is light or heavy. Shellac varnishes containing water or alcohol form a hard surface which will stand a lot of retouching, while so-called matting varnishes containing gum dammar and turpentine will permit only a limited amount of treatment.

Types of Varnish

Varnishes can be bought ready prepared or made up according to the following formulae.

We distinguish between water, warm alcohol and cold varnishes.

VARNISHING

Before retouching negatives with pencil they must be varnished to provide a surface which will take the pencil work.

1. Matt varnish and common retouching media are applied by means of a linen cloth.

2. Place the negative emulsion upon a flat surface.

3. Dip the cloth into a small quantity of the varnish.

4. Rub it on evenly with a circular motion.

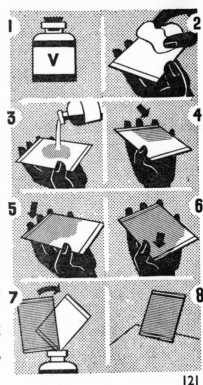

1. To protect the negative and at the same time provide a retouching surface, hot or cold negative varnishes can be used.

2. Before applying the varnish, clean and thoroughly dry the negative.

3. Pour a pool of the varnish on to the centre of the negative.

4. Carefully tilt the negative so that the varnish flows towards one corner.

5. Tilt it in the opposite direction to cover the second corner.

6. Continue in this way until the film of varnish covers the whole surface.

7. Drain off the surplus liquid from the last corner back into the bottle.

8. Stand the plate up to dry.

R.—E

10.—WATER VARNISH

Borax	¾ ounce	20 grams
Water	40 ounces	1,000 c.cm.
Shellac	3¼ ounces	80 grams

Dissolve the borax in the water, bring to the boil, and add the shellac in small quantities. Continue boiling until all the shellac is completely dissolved.

The negative can be bathed in this varnish. After drying it will have a matt coating which easily takes retouching. Water varnish is not, however, recommended if the negative is to be considerably enlarged.

11.—WARM ALCOHOL VARNISH FOR PLATES

Bleaches shellac (powdered)	4 ounces	100 grams
Gum sandarac	1 ounce	25 grams
Gum mastic	45 grains	2·5 grams
Gum dammar	45 grains	2·5 grams
Castor oil	2 drops	2 drops
Rectified spirit (96% alcohol)	40 ounces	1,000 c.cm.

After everything is dissolved, leave the varnish to stand for a time until the solution is clear. Filter before use. Industrial (colourless) methylated spirit can be used instead of the rectified spirit.

Before using the varnish, warm the plate and pour the varnish over it. If the coating is unsatisfactory, it can be removed by dissolving in alcohol.

12.—COLD VARNISH

Gum dammar	¼ ounce	6 grams
Carbon tetrachloride	4 ounces	100 c.cm.
When dissolved, add		
Manilla copal	¼ ounce	6 grams

Heat the mixture on a water bath, and leave standing moderately warm for several hours. Filter before use.

13.—ALTERNATIVE COLD VARNISH

Gum sandarac	2 ounces	50 grams
Benzene	8 ounces	200 c.cm.
Acetone	10 ounces	250 c.cm.
Rectified spirit (96% alcohol)	5 ounces	125 c.cm.

Leave the mixture standing for some time, shaking occasionally. Industrial (colourless) methylated spirit can be used instead of rectified spirit. Filter before use. If the solution is cloudy add a few pieces of dry silica gel as anhydrous calcium chloride before filtering.

Note.—This mixture is inflammable.

Cold varnishes form a somewhat softer coating than the warm alcohol type, but can stand a good deal of retouching work.

Negatives must be perfectly dry before varnish is applied. The varnish is then poured on, care being taken that the liquid spreads evenly over the whole negative surface. Surplus varnish should be allowed to drip back into the bottle from one corner of the plate, and the latter then placed in a rack to dry.

If only a limited amount of light retouching is needed, as when parts of a negative require a slight strengthening of density, it will be sufficient to prepare the surface with a matting varnish or retouching medium. Suitable preparations of this type are available commercially as retouching media.

Rapid matting varnish dries much faster than the ordinary type, but suffers from the disadvantage that the retouching shows up in enlargement, especially when a condenser-type enlarger is used. Normal and rapid matting varnishes may be prepared from the following formulae :

14.—NORMAL MATTING VARNISH

Gum dammar	1 ounce	25 grams
Oil of turpentine	5 ounces	125 c.cm.

15.—RAPID MATTING VARNISH

Gum dammar	$\frac{1}{2}$ ounce	12 grams
Spirits of turpentine	3 ounces	75 c.cm.
Petrol or petroleum ether	3 ounces	75 c.cm.
Oil of lavender	75 drops	75 drops

The rapid varnish is inflammable, but dries rather more quickly than the normal matting varnish.

Whereas other varnishes are poured on to the negative surface, matting varnishes are rubbed in. Place the negative emulsion upwards on the retouching desk. Dip a fine linen cloth, e.g., an old handkerchief, in a small quantity of varnish and rub it evenly over the negative surface. A leather is less suitable than linen, as fragments may come away and cause a smear.

If the negatives are to be printed by contact it is sufficient to apply the matting varnish only to the parts to be retouched. But if they are to be enlarged, it is preferable to coat the whole surface, as otherwise the parts treated will show up ; matting varnish has the property of making the emulsion layer rather more transparent. Apply only a very thin coat so that the surface feels just slightly sticky to the touch. Do not apply more than the emulsion can absorb ; if the coating is too thick, remove it with a pad of cotton wool soaked in turpentine or petrol.

As an alternative to retouching the negative, a sheet of matt film may be laid over it and worked on instead. Matt film has a slightly grainy surface, like films with matt backing, which is suitable for pencil work.

IV—VARNISHES AND RETOUCHING MEDIA

Make	Negative Varnish	Matt Varnish	Retouching Medium
Autotype			Retouching medium
Faber	Mattolein		
Günther Wagner	Pelikan retouching varnish		
Hailie	Mattolein		
Ilford			Retouching medium
Johnsons	Crystal varnish Dammar varnish Negative varnish White hard varnish	Ivorex Matt varnish Matt ruby varnish Matt orange varnish	Retouching medium
Kodak	Negative varnish		Special retouching medium
Marabu	Mattolein		
Tetenal	Rapid Mattolein	Matt varnish (colourless, red, green, blue)	Retuschin
Winsor & Newton	W. & N. white spirit varnish Winton retouching varnish	Winton matt varnish	W. & N. retouching varnish

PENCIL WORK

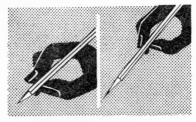

Hold the pencil well back from the point (*right*); a cramped grip near the point (*left*) does not afford sufficiently fine control (p. 98).

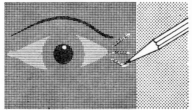

Use the pencil to fill in small light areas on the negative such as facial wrinkles and lines. Fill the area in with small loops or circles. These blend most easily into the image (p. 100).

Resharpen the pencil frequently on a sandpaper block. Rotate the pencil while sharpening (*left*).

After sharpening carefully, wipe the point with cotton wool to remove all graphite dust (*right*).

Do not attempt to apply too much pencil work to any one area or the latter applications will actually decrease the density. This is due to the fact that the pencil point pushes the varnish layer aside instead of depositing more graphite on top of it (p. 126).

Retouching varnishes and media can usually be removed by wiping the negative over with a suitable solvent such as petrol. This also removes the pencil work.

Choice of Pencil

Pencils are available in various grades of hardness, the most useful for retouching purposes being the 4H, 2H, F, HB, and 2B. If the negative is to be considerably darkened, use a soft grade such as HB or 2B. Light retouching is carried out with the harder grades such as 4H ; the harder the pencil, the finer and less visible the work.

The right pencil to use is that which matches the surrounding density after only four or five applications to the same spot. There is a limit to the amount of pencil work that can be done on one place ; density will increase at first, but after six or seven applications of the pencil it will suddenly fall off again. The reason for this falling off is that the pencil point pushes the matting varnish away from the place treated and there is thus no gum layer left on which the graphite can take. Instead, a sticky roll of gum mixed with graphite powder accumulates all round the retouched area.

Once this has happened there is nothing for it but to remove the entire coat of varnish and make a fresh start. Even then there is a risk that the negative, having been polished quite smooth by the preceding treatment, will no longer take the pencil. The thicker the coating of matting varnish, the more likely this is to happen.

Therefore always try out the pencil first on a corner of the negative in order to ascertain whether four or five applications produce sufficient density.

V—RETOUCHING PENCIL LEADS

Make	Grades
A. W. Faber	Castell 4H, 3H, 2H, H, F, HB, B, 2B, 3B, 4B
E. Faber	Van Dyke 4H, 3H, 2H, H, F, HB, B, 2B, 3B, 4B
	Aquarello (positive)
Ilford	2B, B, HB, 4, 2H, 3H, 4H, 5H, 6H
Lyra	Orlov (negative) 4H, 3H, 2H, F, H, HB, B, 2B, 3B, 4B
	Colorida (positive) 1, 2, 3
Schwan	Stabilo Negative B, HB, F, H
	Stabilo Positive 1, 2, 3, 4, 5
Staedtler	Mars H, HB, B (negative) ; 1, 2, 3 (positive)
Venus	2B, B, HB, F, 2H, 3H, 4H, 5H, 6H

Matching Density

In pencil retouching we usually have to match the density of the affected part with the surrounding area ; and this must be done with great accuracy.

Matching is sometimes very difficult when the operator is blinded by the light reflected in the mirror behind the desk. One way of overcoming this drawback and at the same time avoiding eyestrain is to cut a circular hole in a sheet of black paper and place it over the negative so that all but the part under treatment is masked off.

The Correct Pencil Stroke

Hold the pencil lightly, well back from the point. Do not press too hard or the results will be crude, and the fine point will easily break off. Turn the pencil gradually as the point is being worn off. Without lifting the pencil from the negative, draw a series of tiny complete circles or loops evenly over the whole area. Some retouchers prefer to draw a series of small straight lines, but loops are less visible as they imitate the formation of the actual grains of the emulsion. The smaller the loops and the sharper the pencil point, the more successful the work will be.

Sharpening the Point

Sharpen the pencil to a very fine point and frequently resharpen while working. After each resharpening be careful to remove the graphite dust adhering to the point before starting work again, or it will stick to the matting varnish and may form black spots. The pencil point should be so fine that only a little extra pressure would serve to break it.

Grip the pencil lightly, so that it almost drops from the hand. Even when touching out straight lines such as telegraph wires, do not be misled into drawing a straight line with the pencil, but use the same circular stroke, forming a series of tiny loops along the line in question.

Faults and Failures

The newcomer to pencil retouching usually makes the negative defect worse than before, and this is due to lack of practice. We therefore recapitulate the commonest causes of failures :

Varnish coating too thick.
Pencil too hard or too soft.
Pencil point not sharp enough.
Pencil strokes too coarse.
Pencil pressed too hard.

Pencil marks can be removed with petrol or turpentine in the event of mistakes. However, in spite of the coating of matting varnish every pencil stroke tends to polish the otherwise somewhat rough surface of the emulsion, for the varnish is not hard enough to protect the gelatine. Each time the pencil is used, the surface therefore becomes smoother and less able to take further treatment.

It is thus wrong to retouch carelessly in the belief that mistakes can always be washed away. There are limits to what can be done, and it is advisable to get to know these limits from the start.

RETOUCHING ON THE BACK

Though the methods to be described are partly obsolete to-day, they are mentioned here for the sake of completeness and because they can still occasionally be used with profit. Only a few years ago they were indispensable, and many old photographers still adopt them. For copying purposes their usefulness remains undiminished.

The disadvantage with all these methods is that negatives will stand little or no enlargement after treatment.

Thus holding back portions so as to lighten the corresponding areas of the print (p. 70) can equally be carried out on the back of the negative.

The treatment of films (other than miniature films) differs in no way from that already described. Neo-coccine may, for instance, be applied to either side, as both have a gelatine coating.

With plates a different procedure is required, as the dye will not take on glass. Red water colour paint, such as madder, can, it is true, be used to paint over certain parts of a negative to make them print lighter, as this paint is made up with a binding agent which adheres to glass. But a completely uniform coating is unobtainable ; dark edges form and render the negative unsuitable for enlarging. In contact printing, however, the thickness of the glass mitigates the unduly sharp outline of the paint.

Matt Varnish

To prepare the back of a plate for retouching, a matt varnish is used. When poured over the glass it leaves a matt, slightly grainy surface which readily takes water-colour paint and permits pencil work. Matt varnish may be made up according to the following formulae :

16.—MATT VARNISH FOR PLATES

Gum sandarac	175	grains	10	grams
Gum mastic	45	grains	2·5	grams
Ether	4	ounces	100	c.cm.
Benzene	1½	ounces	38	c.cm.

Increased benzene content produces a finer surface grain.

17.—ALTERNATIVE MATT VARNISH

Gum sandarac	80	grains	5	grams
Gum dammar	60	grains	3·5	grams
Ether	2½	ounces	63	c.cm.
When dissolved, add :				
Benzene	2	ounces	50	c.cm.
Alcohol	2–10	drops	2–10	drops

Increased alcohol content produces finer surface grain.

Both varnishes require the addition of a few drops of water as they otherwise do not form a matt surface.

Pour the matt varnish over the back of the plate in the same way as cold varnish (p. 123).

Those who do not care to work with these solutions, which are highly inflammable, may prefer to buy ready prepared varnish.

Holding Back with Graphite

After varnishing the back of the negative, apply graphite powder over the thin parts with a piece of chamois leather.

As some difficulty may be found in applying the powder evenly to a large area, it is better in such a case to reverse the procedure, covering the whole negative with graphite, and lighten the dense areas. This is achieved either by scraping away the varnish at the appropriate places with a retouching knife or removing it with a wiper dipped in alcohol. An alternative method is to paint cold varnish (see p. 122) over the matt varnish ; this will render it transparent.

If the effect obtained is still insufficient, add a dye, such as quinoline yellow or congo red to a varnish and pour on a fresh coating. When dry, remove the dye from the dense parts of the negative. If removal of the varnish leaves a border which shows up in printing, the edge can be shaded in by the use of a retouching knife.

Instead of varnishing, a sheet of special matt film can be laid against the back of the negative and worked on with wiper and graphite powder, exactly as described above. The matt film must be firmly stuck to the four corners of the plate so as to prevent it slipping during printing.

Matt film can also be rubbed all over with graphite powder. Dense parts of the negative emulsion underneath are then lightened with an erasing knife or plastic rubber. It is also possible to lighten larger areas not covered with graphite by painting them over with a suitable oil to make them transparent.

Ordinary white paper, or tissue paper can be used instead of matt film, though it gives a coarser grain. Alternatively, spray the glass back evenly by an air brush (see p. 165) and wipe clean those parts which print too light with an ordinary brush and water.

Holding Back with Pigment

The halo effect so popular in portraiture, i.e., the white rim round the face contour that merges into the background, can be obtained either with an air brush or by rubbing graphite on the back of the varnished negative.

We can obtain a somewhat coarser halo effect with a bromoil brush by applying some carmine on both sides of the negative near the head, then spreading it by dabbing evenly with the brush. If the paint dries too quickly, it can be moistened by breathing on it. The last stage in this method is to wash away any paint that has spread on to the face by means of a brush dipped in water. As it is important to retain the detail in the features, the treatment should be confined to the borders of the image.

Blocking Out

As its name indicates, this process involves covering over parts of a negative so that they do not print at all. It is very important in colour photography and indispensable in photo-montage work.

Blocking out media are also frequently applied to the back of the film or plate. When printing in clouds from a second negative, the background of the first negative often has to be blocked out.

One way of doing this is to paint over the background with commercial blocking out medium, which is completely opaque when thinly applied. But the result is seldom satisfactory, for blocking out medium has no half-tones ; it either blocks out completely or not at all. Everywhere that the medium forms an outline, the contrast is so sharp and immediate that the print appears to have been cut along it with scissors. As the definition of a negative is rarely sharp enough to bear comparison with such an outline, the contour of the opaque medium consequently looks unnatural. Some shading of the outline is therefore necessary, and this can be done in one of two ways.

Softening the Outline

To block out a plate negative which is to be printed by contact, add red pigment or asphalt varnish to a matt varnish so as to render it opaque. Coat the back of the plate with this mixture.

Then remove the varnish from those parts of the image which are to be retained, by scraping away with a knife or wiping with a piece of cotton wool soaked in alcohol. The thicker the glass base, the softer the outlines of the image will be when printed.

This method is unsuitable for negatives which are to be enlarged, as the outline of the varnish on the back of the plate would appear too sharp in the enlargement.

Film negatives cannot be blocked out in this way, even

BLOCKING OUT

To block out plate negatives proceed as follows :

1. Prepare a mixture of matt varnish with red or black pigment.

2. Paint this mixture over the back of the negative.

3. Scrape away the pigment from those parts of the negative which are to be reduced.

4. Alternatively wash off the varnish layer in those places with a suitable solvent.

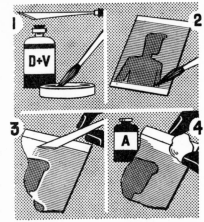

1. With film negatives no varnish is used but only dye.

2. Carefully apply a border of black or red retouching dye round the outlines of the subject.

3. Soften the actual outline with a brush charged with water.

4. On the back of the negative fill in the area beyond the border with Indian ink or opaque.

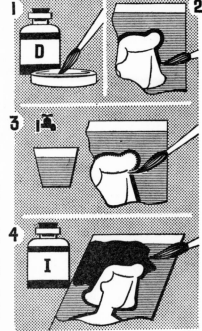

133

if they are only to be printed by contact. Knife work on the back of a film is, of course, in any case quite out of the question. A different method is required, the work being carried out initially on the emulsion side.

Preparing a Dye Border

The first step is to paint a border about $\frac{1}{8}$ inch wide round the outline of the part of the image which is to remain, using black retouching dye. The dye, as opposed to opaque pigment, does cover on the first application, but becomes increasingly dense the more often we paint over the same area.

Continue applying the dye with the brush until the border becomes really opaque. Do not follow the outline exactly, but work the brush sometimes a little beyond it and sometimes not as far, so as to soften the edge.

As small drops of blocking out medium are formed at the point where the brush is lifted from the surface, the brush stroke must finish well within the border, not at its edge, when painting over the outline.

As soon as the border is sufficiently dense, wash round its inner edge with a brush dipped in plain water. Here again the brush strokes must be made from the outline of the image into the border, and not the other way round. Continue washing until the inner edge of the border is sufficiently soft.

Filling in the Background

After drying, fill in the remainder of the background with opaque pigment, but leave at least $\frac{1}{16}$ inch of the original border untouched. Any subsequent correction of the border that may be necessary can then be made without running the brush into the blocking out medium.

With films, the first stage of blocking out is again carried out on the emulsion side, but for the final filling-in

134

of the background, it is better to work on the back. There is then no danger of accidentally getting blocking out medium on the brush when correcting the border. The image in a negative treated in this manner has a soft outline and will stand almost any degree of enlargement.

DAMAGED NEGATIVES

Dealing with Scratches

However much care is taken, negatives sometimes get scratched ; miniature and roll films are particularly susceptible. The smaller the negative size, the more serious the consequences.

Smaller scratches sometimes disappear in enlargement if the procedure for suppressing grain, described on p. 141, is adopted.

Scratches can sometimes be removed from the film by polishing with silver polishing powder or jeweller's rouge. Take a quantity of powder on a wad of cotton wool and spread it evenly over the emulsion side, then polish until the film is quite smooth again. If the scratches are not too deep they usually disappear, but if not, polish the film once again. Even if they are not entirely eliminated, the polishing will make them less prominent by smoothing down the texture of the scratch.

Scratches show up badly when the negative is enlarged in a condenser-enlarger fitted with a point source of light (e.g., a projector-type lamp). The light rays are scattered by the scratches, which form miniature hollows in the gelatine layer, and thus become apparent.

By preventing such scattering we can largely conceal damage to the film surface. This is achieved by placing a small quantity of liquid having roughly the same refractive index as gelatine on the film, and then sandwiching the film between two glass plates. Any kind of fine oil is suitable, also glycerine or carbon tetrachloride. Use enough liquid to exclude all air from the sandwich.

The resulting surface is optically almost flat, so that refraction can no longer take place at the damaged place.

NEGATIVE FLAWS

To eliminate scratches on films, bind up the negative between two sheets of glass with a small quantity of fine oil between the surfaces (p. 136).

Apply a pool of oil on the first plate, lower the negative over it, apply another pool, and cover with a cover glass. Press the sandwich together first at the centre and then work outwards so as to eliminate all air bubbles. This sandwich can then be enlarged as it stands.

If a plate is broken but the gelatine layer still more or less intact, the negative can be saved by duplication (p. 138).

1. Place the plate in a glassless printing frame.

2. Cover it with a sheet of direct duplicating film.

3. Close the frame carefully but do not apply too much pressure.

4. Turn the frame over and fill in the cracks in the glass with fine oil diluted with petrol.

5. Remove all surplus.

6. Fix four drawing pins to the four corners of the frame and attach a string to each.

7. Suspend the frame by the strings, twisting them up.

8. Hold the whole over the exposing lamp and allow the string to untwist thus spinning the frame and preventing the crack from forming shadows on the film.

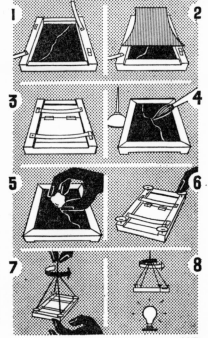

R.—F

Most small scratches will completely disappear and larger ones appear much reduced.

Alternatively, we can produce a new non-refracting surface by varnishing the emulsion layer. Treat the damaged parts with a varnish composed of pyroxyline and amyl acetate with an equal volume of glacial acetic acid and applied with a fine hair brush.

Ready-made protective film varnishes and scratch-proofing preparations as used in the motion picture industry are equally suitable.

Broken Plates

Plates may suffer yet another kind of damage : breakage of the glass base. If the film is torn in the process, there is nothing to be done ; but if it is undamaged, we can save the plate by making a duplicate negative. This must, of course, be done in a darkroom.

Lay the plate gently in a printing frame from which the glass has been removed, then place a sheet of direct duplicating film over the negative and close the frame carefully. If the printing frame has strong springs, these may have to be bent back to reduce the pressure.

Turn over the printing frame. By the light of the safelight and with the aid of a brush, paint in the crack from the front with a mixture of equal parts of pure colourless sewing machine oil and petrol. As soon as the crack is completely filled in, i.e., when it has almost disappeared, remove the surplus oil with a cloth.

Next take four drawing pins and insert one in each corner of the frame. Attach a piece of string to each, gather the strings together in one hand and spin the frame with the other so as to wind them together like a rope. Hold the frame so that it does not unwind.

To make the exposure, hold the printing frame suspended over an electric bulb by the strings, switch on and allow the frame to spin like a top as the string unwinds. The spinning movement diffuses the light so that the image of the crack in the glass is not reproduced on the positive.

Direct duplicating film develops to another negative, and the printing method described above should eliminate very nearly all traces of the crack in the original negative. Any mark remaining can be almost entirely touched out by pencil.

If direct duplicating film is not available, an intermediate positive can be made on a lantern plate and the duplicate negative printed from this.

MINIATURE NEGATIVES

With miniature negatives it is more important than ever to avoid the necessity of retouching, and in particular of spotting. By meticulous cleanliness in handling it is perfectly possible to prevent dust particles from getting on the film. At the considerable degree of enlargement to which such negatives are subjected, every dust particle is greatly magnified and becomes very noticeable. Any attempt at spotting, however fine the work, would be equally visible, and is therefore out of the question as far as the negative is concerned.

However, provided that the work is carried out with almost microscopic precision, it is quite possible to use almost all other methods of retouching on miniature negatives.

Essential Equipment

Manual skill is the first requirement ; the second is a suitable magnifier. An ordinary reading glass giving a 2 times magnification is sometimes sufficient.

One way of fixing a magnifier so as to leave both hands free, is to fill a pot with sand and stick the handle in it in the desired position. In this way the glass can be set at almost any angle in front of the retouching desk.

Stand magnifiers are, of course, more convenient, as they allow the hands more freedom of movement. Watchmaker's magnifiers are even better, as they enlarge the negative considerably ; but the head must be held close to the desk when using them.

Work on the Negative

Pencil retouching of a miniature portrait negative presents no particular difficulty. The head is likely to occupy a space of at least $\frac{3}{8}$ inches square, which is large enough to permit pencil work on the features. With a light touch and a 2 or 3 times magnifier, retouching a miniature negative is not greatly different from working on quarter plate size.

Holding back presents no special problems either for miniature workers, for the dye has no distinctive texture. If a sufficiently small brush is used, small negative areas can be tackled with confidence.

When working with the face close to the negative, there is a danger of softening the gelatine by continually breathing on it, and so rendering it liable to damage. The remedy is to fold a piece of paper in two and hold it between the teeth so as to deflect the breath away from the emulsion layer.

To protect the negative from fingerprints, cut a triangular hand-rest out of cardboard and stick a piece of chamois leather to the underside. The right hand rests on top while the leather presses the film against the glass plate.

With these precautions a skilled retoucher can obtain thoroughly satisfactory results on miniature negatives. Further retouching can, however, still be carried out on an enlarged intermediate negative (p. 144).

Suppressing Grain

Coarse grain is the bogey of every miniature worker, particularly when we use high-speed films or over-develop the negative. The graininess really shows up on enlargement. The coarser the grain, the lower the magnification at which it becomes apparent. The phenomenon of graininess is observed when negatives are enlarged. It is most objectionable over large areas of uniform density, e.g., in the sky. It follows that the easiest way to avoid grain is to limit the degree of enlargement.

Grain shows up most strongly when the negative is printed on glossy paper ; on a rough surfaced paper the surface tends to mask the grain of the negative. Therefore do not use glossy-surfaced papers for grainy negatives.

Graininess is also affected by the type of enlarger illumination. Condenser-enlargers fitted with a point source or projector lamp tend to accentuate grain.

Enlargers with diffused lighting will considerably reduce the effect of grain. When working with a condenser-enlarger, therefore, place a sheet of opal glass between the lamp and the condenser, or use an opal enlarger lamp.

Soft-Focus Methods

While the above precautions provide the best means of obtaining a reasonably grainless enlargement, there are other special methods of suppressing grain, all of which, however, entail a loss of sharpness in the print.

Thus a piece of fabric such as tulle or crepe georgette will diffuse the image slightly and thus also destroy graininess. We can stretch the material on a cardboard frame and hold it between the lens and the printing paper or fix it over the enlarger lens by a rubber band. The lighter the colour of the material, the softer and more diffused the resulting print will be.

Soft focus attachments will work in the same way (see also p. 49). These are discs usually inscribed with a series of concentric circles which refract the light rays and thus soften the image.

Another means of softening definition is to take a sheet of plain glass and rub a trace of grease over it in rings. If we want to retain a sharp image while adding a little diffusion, we can divide the exposure into two parts, the soft-focus attachment being used for the second part only. Special enlarging lenses are also designed for suppression of grain by optical means ; they are imperfectly corrected in the same way as soft-focus camera lenses (p. 49). The degree of diffusion given by such a lens is regulated by the iris diaphragm.

SUPPRESSING GRAIN

The type of enlarger used may affect the degree to which grain shows up.

Condenser enlargers with a point source reproduce every smallest detail of the negative (left). Modern semi-diffused enlargers tend to suppress extremely fine detail such as grain.

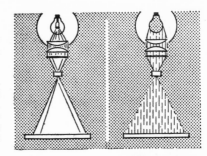

Diffusion by means of soft focus attachments over the enlarger lens will also tend to suppress grain (p. 142).

1. The subject photographed by the camera produces

2. a sharp image.

3. During enlargement the soft focus attachment spreads the shadows of the image

4. into the light highlight areas.

A diffusion attachment can consist of a piece of silk stretched over a frame (left) or concentric circles engraved on a piece of glass or plastic (right). A homemade variation is a glass plate smeared with circles of vaseline (centre).

With the circular diffusion disc the degree of softness depends on the aperture of the enlarger lens. At small apertures the lens includes few circles and the image is sharper (left). At larger apertures the effective lens diameter includes more circles and the image becomes softer.

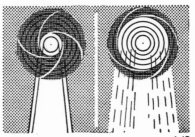

143

Making a Duplicate

We can considerably reduce graininess by preparing an intermediate enlarged negative which is used in turn for making very big enlargements.

First make an enlarged positive transparency, e.g., quarter-plate or 4 × 5 inches. However, expose through the glass back instead of direct on to the emulsion.

Process the plate in an energetic developer so that the image does not penetrate very deeply into the emulsion layer.

The light rays, passing through the glass base, form an image on the underside of the emulsion and are then diffused in their progress towards the top surface. As development proceeds in the opposite direction, the developer first attacks those parts of the emulsion affected by the more diffused rays.

If the developer were to work through to the bottom of the emulsion, it would reach those parts of the image that are sharp and free from diffusion. But that would not achieve the desired effect.

By confining development to the top layer of the emulsion, we therefore obtain a transparency in which the image consists not of the silver grains first affected by the exposure, but of those which form the diffused image to produce uniform densities.

The next step is to make the new intermediate negative by printing from the transparency. The final enlargement is then made from this negative. Some loss of sharpness is inevitable in the process, and it is necessary to decide whether to retain maximum definition, or to sacrifice it for the sake of suppressing graininess.

Redevelopment

With negatives which are somewhat contrasty and can stand some reduction of gradation, graininess may be reduced by bleaching and redevelopment.

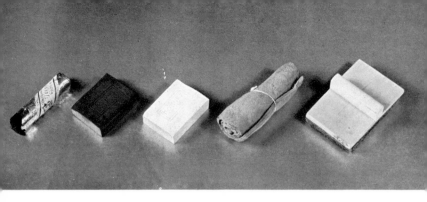

CRAYON WORK. Crayons and chalks can be applied direct or with stumps (*above*) to matt prints. The chalk is rubbed on a felt pad and carefully wiped over the print (*below left*) to lighten up or darken larger areas. For oil crayons (p. 159) the print surface is first treated with a suitable medium and drawn over with the crayon (*below right*). For soft outlines the crayon work may be smudged up with a stump.

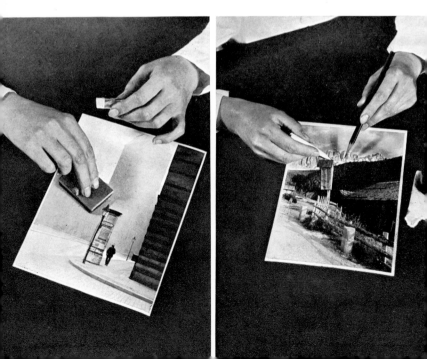

REMOVING BLACK SPOTS. On prints this involves careful scraping with a retouching knife. The spot should slowly blend into its surroundings, and not be scratched out in one go.

PRESSURE MARKS, " Tram lines " and similar marks can be removed in the same way, gradually working along the line from end to end (p. 157).

SPOTTING PRINTS. The easiest and quickest method is to use pigment or water colour matched to the density of the surrounding tone. One dab with the brush should fill the spot (p. 157).

DYE RETOUCHING. On prints, dyes allow treatment of larger portions ; the dye is applied in washes, building up density where required (p. 160).

CUT-OUTS. Prints with a completely white background can be produced by bleaching out the unwanted parts with Farmer's reducer (p. 58), painted on with a brush.

EXTENSIVE PRINT RETOUCHING may involve the use of dye or black crayon to deepen the shadows, and scraping to brighten highlights (*opposite*). Usually this amount of work shows appreciably on the print which may need rephotographing.

On Page 152 : VARNISHING. Some varnishes may be applied by pouring them over the print (*top left*). Often it is more convenient to spray them on with a blower or spray gun (p. 163).

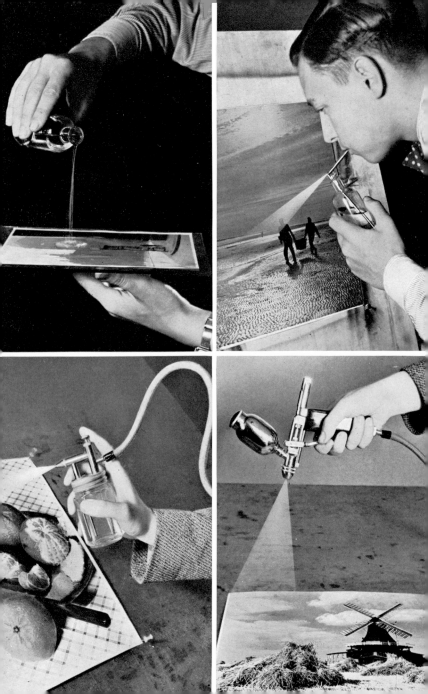

18.—BLEACHING BATH

Copper sulphate crystals	1 ounce	25 grams
Sodium chloride	1 ounce	25 grams
Sulphuric acid, 10% solution	2½ ounces	62 c.cm.
Water to make	10 ounces	250 c.cm.

After bleaching, rinse for 15 minutes and redevelop in the following developer :

19.—REDEVELOPER FOR FINE GRAIN

Para-phenylene diamine	50 grains	3 grams
Sodium sulphite, anhyd.	1 ounce	25 grams
Water to make	40 ounces	1,000 c.cm.

Ready prepared fine grain developers may also be used.

On no account develop the negative to finality ; as soon as sufficient density is reached, give it a quick rinse and fix in acid fixing bath.

While in the fixer the negative will lose density and become notably softer, while the reduction in graininess will also be noticeable. Do not, however, shorten the re-development so much that the negative becomes too soft to print on any but extra-hard paper.

PRINT RETOUCHING

Unless a print is to be copied or reproduced photo-mechanically, handwork is normally limited to spotting. While careful spotting can be virtually undetectable, more extensive work on the lines of that described in the preceding chapters is immediately apparent. The surface of the paper is almost invariably discoloured, roughened or made smoother by such handwork, and it is only when rephoto-graphed, as with a process camera for block-making purposes, that the signs of after-treatment disappear.

Apart from spotting, the various other retouching methods described in the following pages, therefore, have their main value in preparing prints for reproduction.

After-treatment of Prints

Chemical after-treatment similar to that used for negatives can also be carried out on prints.

There is, however, one important difference. Whereas it is immaterial whether the tone of a negative changes after treatment, the tone of a print must remain constant ; for obvious reasons we can tolerate no blue or brown discoloration. Local reduction can therefore only be carried out with solutions that do not change the colour of the print. Local intensification is ruled out altogether, as a change of colour always takes place. This is, however, no great loss, as we should have sufficient control over the enlarging process to make local intensification unnecessary.

Local reduction may be necessary to lighten shadows that have become completely blocked up. A suitable reducing agent, which does not change the colour of the print, is potassium permanganate.

PRINT RETOUCHING

Spots or excessively deep shadows on prints can be treated by local reduction with permanganate reducer (p. 156). This must be followed by a fixing bath.

For yellow developer stains a thiocarbamide clearing bath may be used (p. 156).

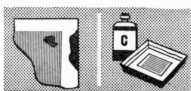

The amount of retouching that can be done on prints depends on the print surface. Matt prints will stand up to dye and pigment retouching, scraping, pencil work and even treatment with chalks (p. 157).

On semi-matt prints the areas retouched must be suitably treated to match the sheen of the surrounding surface. This is done by means of gum. Semi-matt papers can also be worked up with oil crayons for which purpose the surface is first rubbed over with a mixture of turpentine and linseed oil.

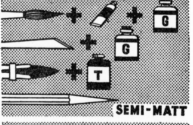

Glossy prints can be successfully retouched only with dye.

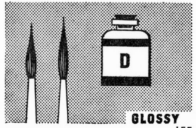

20.—POTASSIUM PERMANGANATE REDUCER

A. Potassium permanganate	70 grains	4 grams
Water	40 ounces	1,000 c.cm.
B. Sulphuric acid, 10% solution	1 ounce	25 c.cm.
Water to make	40 ounces	1,000 c.cm.

For use mix 3 parts each of A and B, and make up to 100 parts with water.

Place the wet print on a sheet of glass and wipe the parts to be reduced with a wad of cotton wool or a brush soaked in reducer. The paper base turns brown in the process, but will clear in an acid fixing bath or a 5 per cent solution of potassium metabisulphite.

The reducer works slowly but care is needed to ensure that it does not flow over parts of the print which should not be reduced.

Farmer's reducer is not very suitable, as the image itself tends to acquire a violet stain. It can, however, be used in certain circumstances. When copying line drawing, the background often shows a slight veil, which is, in fact, a faint silver deposit. This can be removed with a wad of cotton wool soaked in Farmer's reducer. Here there is no danger of staining, as we are completely dissolving away the silver in the veiled areas, so that only pure gelatine remains.

In the same way Farmer's reducer may be used on normal prints to produce a pure white area.

Removing Stains

Yellow stains caused by exhaustion of the fixing bath or by unduly prolonged development can be removed by wiping over with Farmer's reducer. This works with stains at the edge of the print or outside dense parts of the image. If they are in the middle of the image, use a thiocarbamide clearing bath, which does not attack the blackened silver.

21.—THIOCARBAMIDE CLEARING BATH

Thiocarbamide	1 ounce	25 grams
Citric acid crystals	½ ounce	12·5 grams
Water to make	40 ounces	1,000 c.cm.

Clearing takes about 5 minutes. If the print is left for longer in the solution slight reduction will result. Yellow stains usually disappear of their own accord if the print is first bleached and then toned brown in sodium sulphide.

Dry Retouching on Prints

Prints and enlargements often show small but disturbing blemishes which we have to remove.

Dust particles adhering to the negative during enlargement or falling on the paper itself will cause small white spots. Mistakes in negative retouching may require correction on the print.

In order to make a presentable print, the remedy in both cases is spotting. The procedure varies according to the surface of the paper.

Matt Surfaces

Nearly all matt-surfaced papers are similar to artist's drawing or water-colour paper and can be drawn or painted on as well as treated with a knife. When using pigment, bear in mind that photographic paper has a top coating of gelatine which requires special brush technique (p. 78).

Black spots on a matt print can easily be scraped away with a sharp knife. Owing to the dull finish, the scraping will scarcely be noticeable and the surface will hardly change its appearance at all. It is even safe to tackle larger surfaces, and use the knife to strengthen highlights.

Pinholes are removed with special water colour pigment. Special pigments are supplied for spotting both matt surfaced and glossy prints.

A convenient way to match the pigment to the print colour is to use a small white palette and dilute the various colours separately with water, then prepare the desired shade from the appropriate mixture. A clean piece of glass with a piece of white paper stuck on the underside will also serve the purpose.

As the bromide paper has a gelatine coating it is impor-

157

tant to see that this does not swell unduly during treatment. To prevent swelling, keep the brush as dry as possible and stipple the pigment on in a series of tiny dots, one beside the other. Take care not to touch any place more than once, as otherwise there is a danger of smearing the dots already made.

Retouching for Reproduction

Matt surfaces are used in preference to others when very heavy retouching is required for reproduction purposes. In this case there are a number of other suitable media besides pigments.

Highlights can be strengthened with process white or white poster paint. To have any covering power, this has to be applied fairly thickly, and will stand out in relief on the surface of the paper. For reproduction purposes this is however of no consequence.

Matt papers may also be treated with the retouching pencil. Ordinary graphite pencils are, however, useless, as they leave a shiny mark which would appear lighter than the surrounding area when reproduced. Black chalk or crayon is suitable for matt papers, as it leaves a perfectly dull surface.

Special positive retouching pencils may also be used and are available in various grades of hardness. The softer the grade the deeper the tone obtainable (p. 126).

Areas drawn or shaded over take on a slight sheen, but this is not so strong as to be noticeable in reproduction. Large areas can be treated with artist's chalk, this being wiped over the parts to be treated with a stump of leather cloth. White chalk uniformly lightens the parts treated, black chalk darkens them heavily.

If it is necessary to follow a sharp outline, cut a mask out of cellophane or thin tracing paper and hold it over those parts of the image which are not to be treated. Hold the chalk over the mask and draw it across on to the print ; do not work from the print towards the mask.

If a print has already been painted with process white or worked on with a knife the use of chalk is ruled out. The chalk adheres firmly to the parts already treated and thus shows up the previous work.

Semi-Matt Papers

Spotting of semi-matt or velvet surfaces cannot be carried out with matt surface retouching pigment, as the work would be visible. We need special glossy retouching colours, and as with matt surfaces the spotting brush should be as dry as possible. If the colours themselves dry too matt, they can be mixed with gum arabic. Place a drop of the gum on the palette beside the various colours, mix to the desired tone, then dip the brush in gum before starting work.

Retouching dyes (pp. 75–76) on the other hand, leave no mark on the surface of the print, but sink into the emulsion.

Special positive retouching pencils can also be used to touch up blurred outlines in a print. Provided the pencil is not too hard, the slight sheen will not show up on the semi-matt paper and the handwork will not be apparent. To get a dark tone, therefore, use a softer retouching pencil rather than work over the surface repeatedly with a hard pencil, as this makes it glossy. The pencil should be soft enough to give the correct tone after only one or two applications.

For heavy pencil work oil crayons can be used. First prepare the surface by rubbing it over with a mixture of linseed oil and turpentine. Then colour it with the appropriate pencil and spread the pigment with a paper stump. This produces a smooth even coating in which we can control outlines and transitions of tones. After treatment, hang up the print to dry ; the turpentine will evaporate and the linseed oil forms a dry, resinous surface.

Black spots on a semi-matt print present a problem, as knife work leaves noticeable dull marks on the surface.

One way of overcoming the difficulty is to varnish or wax the print after treatment. Another method is to match the gloss of the surrounding surface by brushing the retouched parts over with a weak solution of gum arabic, diluted isinglass, Scotch glue or one of the proprietary glues. The glues are better, but as they contain a small proportion of acid they will in time cause stains on the print. To neutralize the acid, dissolve a piece of ordinary chalk in the solution and leave it until bubbles have ceased rising to the surface. Once dissolved, the chalk effectively counteracts the acidity.

Glossy Surfaces

Glossy papers are the hardest to work on, for they show up retouching faults mercilessly. It is by no means easy to render handwork on glossy prints undetectable.

Knife work is altogether ruled out, for there is no known means of repairing damage caused to the glazed surface by the knife. It follows from this that all pinholes should be carefully spotted out of the negative with dye. It is better to apply too much than too little, for if a pinhole has been filled in too darkly on the negative, it will print out lighter than its surroundings, and can easily be spotted out again.

Shading with positive retouching pencils is also out of the question, as the pencil will not take on the glossy surface. Spotting with dye remains the only practicable retouching method.

Dyes mixed with a good proportion of gum arabic are often recommended for spotting purposes. But the work is fairly noticeable, and this for obvious reasons. To ensure that a gloss forms on gum arabic when dry it is necessary to use a fair amount of water ; and water is the greatest enemy of a good glazed surface. So all surfaces that come in contact with water lose gloss. The only occasion when dyes should be mixed with gum arabic is when very dense retouching is required. In all other cases it is best to use dyes alone.

With a transparent dye, spotting will not show at all.

These dyes are known as photo tints and are used for colouring photographs, and particularly for colouring glossy prints before glazing. They are usually brownish or bluish in colour, and the right shade can be obtained by mixing different colours. Though they can be used immediately after dilution, the work is even less noticeable if they are first allowed to dry out on the palette before use.

To avoid softening the paper surface and destroying the natural glaze, it is obviously important to keep the brush as dry as possible.

Application of dyestuffs demands a different technique from that required when using water-colour paints. When spotting large areas do not stipple the surface with a series of small dots, one beside the other ; brush it over with a thin solution of dye in one stroke and repeat the process until the right shade is reached.

The glazed surface of the print is easily damaged and requires most careful handling. Inadvertently touching it with the fingers may leave an indelible mark, and it is a useful precaution always to place a sheet of paper under the hand when working.

Varnishing Prints

Often a print which appears thoroughly satisfactory in tone range and depth of shadows when examined while still in the fixing bath, seems to lose brilliance on drying.

It is well known that a print becomes darker as it dries. Hence it is necessary so to regulate enlarging exposure and development that the print appears rather too light when wet, and only takes on the right tone when dry. While glossy papers merely darken as they dry, semi-matt and matt surfaces additionally suffer a flattening of gradation. The image appears to sink into the paper, and the result compares unfavourably with the appearance when wet.

In all such cases after-treatment of the surface by waxing or varnishing can restore the original character of the print. Preparations for the purpose are available commercially as various print varnishes or " dopes," or can be prepared at home. Waxing is analogous to polishing a floor, doping to varnishing furniture.

22.—WAX POLISH FOR PRINTS

White wax	4 ounces	100 grams
Oil of turpentine	4 ounces	100 grams
Gum dammar	70 grains	4 grams

Apply a very thin layer to the print, then polish with fine flannel until the shadows appear fully saturated. The surface, of course, takes on a high polish.

Wax polishing also gives a protection against deterioration by atmospheric action, this being of special value in the case of toned prints, which normally have a short life unless the surface is sealed air-tight.

A still higher polish and a consequent strengthening of the shadows and general increase of brilliance is obtained by varnishing. Varnishes can be poured, painted or sprayed on to the print ; the latter process gives the more even coating.

23.—GLOSSY VARNISH

Gum dammar	175 grains	10 grams
Ether	3 ounces	75 c.cm.
Petrol	3 ounces	75 c.cm.

Dissolve the resin in the cold, as the mixture is very inflammable.

This varnish can be poured on the print and the surplus allowed to run off. If diluted with an equal quantity of petrol, it can also be applied by brush, provided that the print is not too large. This varnish is not very suitable for spraying, as it is highly inflammable. Drying takes about 24 hours.

24.—SEMI-MATT VARNISH

Gum sandarac	1 ounce	25 grams
Benzene	4 ounces	100 c.cm.
Acetone	4 ounces	100 c.cm.
Rectified spirit (96% alcohol)	2 ounces	50 c.cm.

Industrial methylated (colourless) spirit can be used instead of alcohol.

After dilution the varnish can be poured over the print and the surplus soaked off at the edges with fluffless blotting paper.

Spray Varnishing

A very smooth coating is obtained by spraying on the varnish by means of a small atomizer or spray gun (*not* to be confused with an air brush, which is much smaller and must on no account be used for varnish spraying). Zapon or cellulose varnish is suitable. Zapon varnish needs diluting with an equal volume of acetone or amyl acetate.

Mount the enlargement on a board and lean it against the wall. Spray on the varnish from a distance of about a foot. It will not be possible to cover the whole surface at one time.

When the varnish has been sprayed all over, pause for a few seconds to allow it to dry, then continue spraying. In this way several thin layers are applied, one on top of another, until they finally make a uniform surface.

Any attempt to spray on a thick coating all at once will result in the formation of ridges as continuous spraying causes the droplets of varnish to run together.

Applying varnish by spray requires a good pair of lungs. If the varnish refuses to spray, it is a sign that it requires further thinning.

Spraying Matt

While the varnishes described above serve to increase the brilliance of a semi-matt print, a starch solution will produce the opposite, i.e., a matt effect similar to a water-colour painting.

25.—STARCH SOLUTION

Starch	175 grains	10 grams
Boiling water	20 ounces	500 c.cm.

Mix the starch into a smooth paste with a little water, then pour the boiling water on it. Heat the mixture if necessary, stirring it until it becomes opalescent.

It is best to spray the solution while still warm, as this facilitates atomization. Thin white water-colour dulls the surface even more strongly.

Tinting

A further way of treating prints is to tint the paper base. This must be carried out *before* retouching. Soaking in an infusion of tea or weak coffee will dye the paper surface cream. A very weak solution of red ink will give a slightly reddish tinge. The colouring effect of all dyes varies according to the degree of dilution.

AIR BRUSHING

We have already referred to the use of the air brush. Air brush retouching is in fact one of the more important stages of commercial, industrial, and advertising photography.

Air brushing allows the photographer to concentrate on taking the subject only, without worrying over usually unfavourable surroundings. In addition to providing background, the air brush also cleans up, tones, and improves the appearance of the subject far beyond what would be possible by unaided photography of certain limited areas only. In all cases the work can be made to harmonize with the photographic character of the image so that it is virtually undetectable.

Air Brushes

Air brushes are precision instruments and require careful treatment and maintenance. The complete air brush outfit consists of the air brush itself, which is a small spray-gun, and a compressor or cylinder supplying the compressed air.

The essential components of the air brush are a colour cup, or paint reservoir, fitted with a very fine nozzle. This nozzle is closed by a finely ground needle valve. A small knob operated by one finger draws the needle into the nozzle, regulating the flow of the colour.

Compressed air is forced through a tube-shaped housing surrounding the nozzle, thus drawing the colour with it. The force of the air pressure breaks up the colour into tiny particles. On emerging from the air brush, the paint stream takes on the shape of an expanding cone, with the colour most dense in the centre. Therefore the further the brush is held from the print, the larger and broader the coverage.

Pressure Supplies

Compressed air can be supplied to the brush by various methods. We can use either cylinders of compressed (or even liquid) carbon dioxide. Alternatively electrically driven air-compressors or a hand or foot pump can serve to build up sufficient pressure in a reservoir or air receiver.

As air brush retouching is very delicate work, the hand pump is unsatisfactory, for it is difficult to keep a steady hand after working it. Large firms generally use cylinders or electrically driven compressors. For retouching purposes it makes no difference whether cylinders are charged with air or carbon dioxide.

Carbon dioxide cylinders can be refilled cheaply, an exhausted cylinder being exchanged for a fresh one for the cost of the gas alone. Before connecting the cylinder to the air brush, a special reducing valve must be screwed to the tap. This valve consists essentially of a pressure gauge and regulating cock which can be adjusted so as to release only a small quantity of compressed air. The gauge indicates the pressure at which the air is released ; and the regulating cock should be set so that the gauge reads between 22 and 30 pounds per square inch.

To operate the air brush, open the main cock of the cylinder, set the regulating cock to the correct pressure, and finally open the discharge cock to which the tube is connected. Air does not escape until pressure is applied to the knob on the air brush. To shut the equipment off it is only necessary to close the main cock.

Air Brush Colours

Colours for use in an air brush must be very finely ground, for otherwise large particles may remain in the fine nozzle and block it.

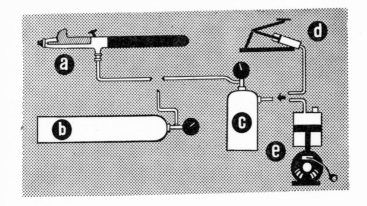

THE AIR BRUSH

Above : The air brush (*a*) blows a mixture of air and fine droplets of colour on to the print. The air supply may be either a cylinder of compressed air (*b*) or a storage container (*c*) into which air is pumped by a foot pump (*d*) or a compressor (*e*) driven by an electric motor.

Below : The air brush itself consists of a reservoir containing the pigment and a finger button controlling a needle valve and the air supply.

Pressing the button (*right*) opens the air valve. Pulling the button backwards also opens the needle valve allowing the colour to flow to the tip of the needle from where it is pulled off in extremely fine droplets by the stream of air rushing past it.

The degree to which the needle is pulled back governs the amount of paint blown out of the air brush. For very fine work and close spraying much less is obviously required than for large areas and broad effects.

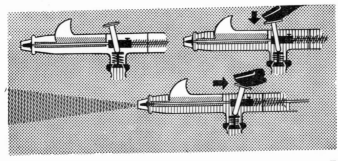

The best paints for air brushing are high-quality water colours or special air brushing paints. When using ordinary water colours, take special care to grind them really smooth and homogeneous.

The colour must be completely dissolved and the solution of even consistency and free of lumps ; the latter must on no account be allowed to get into the air brush colour cup. The cup can either be filled with the aid of a sable brush ; or better still by a dropping-tube, as this eliminates the risk of a stray hair finding its way into the nozzle of the instrument.

Before use these colours must be thinned in water and ground. The degrees of dilution depends on the air pressure to be used. If this is between 22 and 30 pounds per square inch, the colour should be of an oily consistency.

The capacity of the colour cup varies according to the work for which the brush is designed ; it may be anything from 10 minims to ½ ounce of liquid.

The larger instruments are intended for treating large surfaces, though smaller models will serve equally well. So-called spray-guns with large jet and blunt needle valve are much larger and not intended for retouching at all ; they are mainly used for poster work. Their usefulness in the field of photography is confined to the spraying of varnish on to prints (see p. 163).

First class results in air brush retouching are only obtainable if the brush is handled with meticulous care. On no account use any colour other than specially prepared water-colour. Any attempt to use the smaller models of air brush as a varnish spray may ruin the instrument.

Working Procedure

Apart from the obvious desirability of having all necessary equipment within easy reach, it will usually be found best to have the print fastened to an inclined board. If working on a negative (air brush work is usually only done

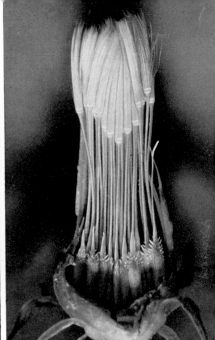

AIR BRUSHING. Spraying with an air brush gives the finishing touch to a print, and can be combined with various other retouching methods to improve detail and depth of tone (*above right*) where it is missing (*above left*).

On Page 170 : AIR BRUSHES. The various designs all incorporate a paint reservoir, a compressed air supply and a needle valve controlled by a press button on top.
The correct hold is a light one (*bottom left*) so that the index finger can easily control the valve.
Generally photographs are air brushed with the help of masks (*bottom right*, see also p. 176), which cover all parts that need no spraying.

On Page 171 : SPRAYING EXERCISES. To get used to handling the air brush, practise spraying first simple shapes with a single mask (*top left*). Then go on to gradations of density, multiple masks (*top right*) and solid shapes (*bottom*).

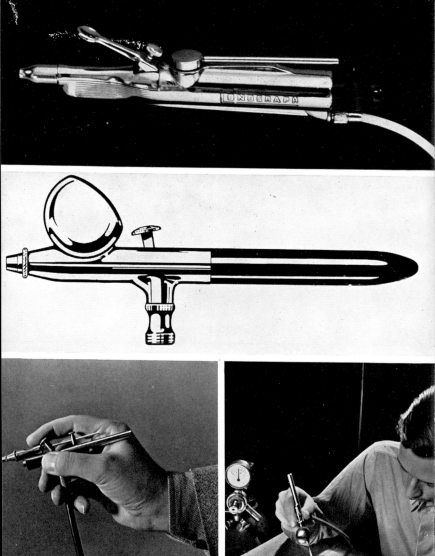

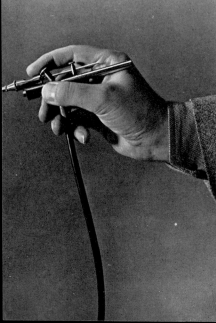

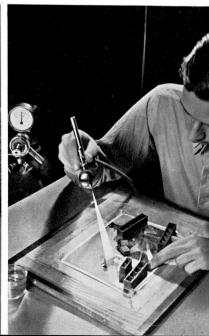

BACKGROUND CONTROL. The airbrush can subdue the surroundings of the subject (*opposite*) and make it stand out or even cover up
disturbing detail such as skirting boards indoors and cast shadows
(*above*). The subject itself is masked either by cut-out masks or by a
resist layer which is afterwards peeled off.

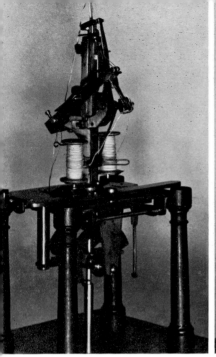

AIR BRUSHING IN INDUSTRY. Straight photographs (*left*) rarely show up machines and components sufficiently clearly in all their detail. These are therefore sprayed—often with the use of many masks—to present the effect familiar from catalogue illustrations of machinery (*right*).

REVERSAL. A picture for reproduction may need reversing left-to-right. There air brushing will obliterate or change inscriptions. To cover up the wording (*left*) it first has to be sprayed white, and then lettered in back-to-front (*right*) before block-making, so that it reads the right way round in the reproduction.

CUTTING MASKS. The tools required are an engraving tool with a rounded edge and a cutting knife (*top*). The contour of the subject area to be masked is then traced through thin celluloid (*below left*) with the engraving tool and cut out with the knife (*below right*). See also p. 179.

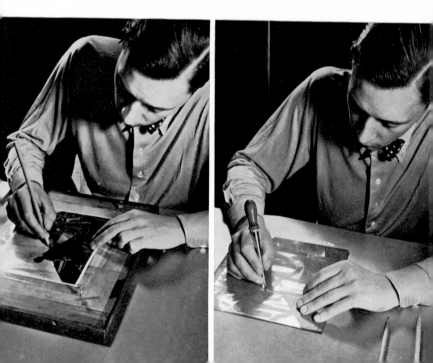

AIR BRUSHING

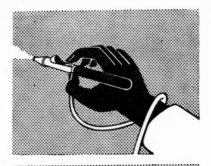

In use hold the air brush lightly in one hand with the index finger on the button and the air supply tube draped round the wrist so that it is out of the way.

To air brush sharp outlines, masks are necessary (p. 179).

1. Prepare the mask by tracing the outlines of the subject on a sheet of cellophane.

2. Cut out the mask along the outline traced.

3. Place it in register over the print and weigh down with small weights or coins.

4. Spray the area round the mask.

The size of the area covered by the spray depends on how far the air brush is from the print surface. For large areas work from further away, for fine details spray from very close up with reduced air pressure.

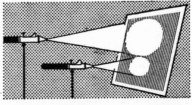

The air brush can also be used to create cloud effects. For this purpose pull a piece of cotton wool into the required shape (*left*) and hold it in position over the picture by means of a fork while spraying round it (p. 182).

on the back), the retouching desk will automatically provide the correct angle.

Sometimes a print cannot be held on a slant and must be laid flat. It will then be necessary to spray from above.

To lighten up a large area evenly, fill the instrument with colour and try out the shade on a piece of paper.

Such a test will also ensure that the print is not spoiled by blobs of colour which are formed when the nozzle is blocked by colour left over from a previous job. The sudden draught of air immediately sucks the particles of colour away from the needle ; this causes further colour to be forced along behind, and the excess forms a blob. Another cause of blobs is a bent needle, which prevents an even flow of liquid from the nozzle, and results in the formation of different sized drops.

When satisfied that the nozzle is emitting an even spray, start on the actual job. Hold the air brush over the surface to be treated, open the air valve cautiously with the index finger and work over the surface with a circular motion until it is evenly covered.

Spray a large surface from a distance, a small area from closer. When working close in, speed is necessary as the narrower the jet the more concentrated it becomes.

Close Spraying

When working close to a print it is important to let the first coat of colour dry before applying a second. If a second coat is sprayed on prematurely, the minute drops of colour of the second application combine with those of the first to form larger, visible drops which make the retouching obvious. Furthermore, the force of the compressed air may blow individual drops right across the surface ; the colour then dries in streaks which show up badly.

Tone Control

The work may well require the brush to be held close to one part and farther away from another part of one and the same print, while maintaining a constant over-all density of colour.

This means that pure colours such as white cannot be used. White should always be mixed with sufficient black to give a shade of grey that remains constant irrespective of the density of the coat. The use of the correct shade of grey is the best way of overcoming the tendency of white colour to glaze the shadow areas of a print, which would make them appear hollow.

Masking

Obviously air brushing permits unlimited shading. To obtain sharp outlines, however, we have to use a mask to cover up those parts of the print which are not to receive any colour.

Masks can be made from various materials such as gelatine, cellophane, thin celluloid, waxed stencil paper, and tinfoil.

Each of these has its advantages and disadvantages. Tinfoil can only be used when there is no need for a transparent mask. When cut straight it is useful for masking in a straight line. Gelatine and cellophane tend to buckle slightly when damp ; and this may or may not be a drawback. Stencil paper on the other hand is not quite transparent.

Cutting the Mask

To prepare a mask, lay the sheet of chosen material over the print and trace the outline of the parts to be covered over, with a sharp-pointed engraver's needle. The rounded point of the needle enables a line to be drawn and at the same time an impression to be cut in any desired direction on the surface of the masking material. The impression then shows up white when the masking sheet is placed on a dark support for cutting out.

Sheet zinc or hardboard are suitable for this purpose. Cut the mask out along the marked line with a stencil knife ground to lancet shape. There is no need to cut right through, for if the knife has gone a certain way, the material will usually break apart.

As we have to hold the mask in place during retouching, it is important when cutting it out to leave wide margins on at least two sides which will extend beyond the edges of the print.

Another way of cutting a mask is to make a duplicate print of the one to be sprayed and cut out the outlines to be masked. The duplicate print, placed in exact register, then forms a perfect mask.

Spraying with the Mask

Once the mask is ready and has been adjusted to fit the necessary outline, fasten it at the outer edges with drawing pins and hold it down with some weights along the outlines to be sprayed. Without these weights, the compressed air will get under the mask and force it up, with the result that colour penetrates underneath. If the outline is fairly straightforward, old toothpaste or adhesives tubes or printer's slugs will serve as weights.

The method just described will be satisfactory if the outline is fairly straightforward, but if it is crooked and zig-zags in and out of the area to be sprayed it is advisable to cut out some narrow tapering strips of cardboard and stick them on the projecting parts of the mask to hold it firm.

If the projections are very sharp, press them down with the point of a knitting needle held in the left hand while spraying the colour with the right. Another way of securing the mask is to coat it underneath with rubber solution, allow time for the solution to become tacky, then stick the mask on the print. It can be pulled away afterwards and all traces of solution rubbed off the print surface.

With the mask in position, spraying of the uncovered

parts of the print can commence. Beginners usually make the mistake of applying too much colour, as the mask conceals those parts not being sprayed. To have a standard comparison, therefore, check the progress of the work by lifting a corner of the mask from time to time.

If the part of the print is too small to be conveniently covered by a mask, a coating of slow-drying linseed oil varnish may be used instead.

26.—AIR BRUSH MASKING VARNISH

Boiled linseed oil	2 parts
Petrol	2 parts
Chalk	1 part

After spraying the colour and allowing it to dry, the varnish, which is waterproof, can be removed without trace, with a wad of cotton wool soaked in petrol.

Multiple Masks

If the shape of the areas to be covered requires the use of more than one mask, these must be applied to the print surface one after the other.

The largest area, or that with the lightest tone, should be covered first, the colour then sprayed round it and the mask removed. Then apply the second mask, similarly treat the surrounding area, and so on until all the print has been properly worked up.

It may prove impossible to mask off small detail in the print such as branches of a tree. In this case it is safe to spray them over together with the background and pick out the detail later with an ordinary brush slightly moistened with water. It is important not to wet the brush too much.

To avoid forming an unsightly rim of colour, start the brush stroke from within the sprayed surface and draw the brush towards the colour-free area ; never work from the unsprayed surface into the colour. At the end of the stroke, mop up the excess colour with a piece of blotting paper and wash the place with fresh water.

Soft Outlines

Masks will only give an absolutely sharp outline if they are completely impervious to water. Gelatine and cellophane are affected by water to the extent of buckling when wet. This property can be turned to good account when we want a soft outline round the areas sprayed.

The procedure is to spray the border over several times in succession. The gelatine meanwhile buckles slightly differently each time, covering up first one part of the border, then another. The different borders that are left after each spraying then overlap and form a soft outline.

To obtain the desired effect it is necessary to hold the nozzle of the air brush over the edge of the mask and direct the spray obliquely across it and on to the uncovered print. If the spray is directed towards the mask from outside, the mask will not stop the colour, which will creep under it.

Spraying-in Clouds

Soft outlines of this kind are appropriate when we want to paint clouds with the air brush. Aesthetically speaking there is little to be said for the process, but the technique is explained here as it has other applications as well.

First prepare a cloud pattern by pulling a wad of cotton wool or piece of coarse blotting paper into the required shape, taking care that the edges are thoroughly frayed.

Place the pattern on the sky portion of the print, holding it in place with a fork or two fingers of the left hand.

Operate the air brush with the right hand, meanwhile moving the cloud pattern very gently to and fro in order to soften the outline.

Dealing with Mistakes

Proficiency with the air brush is only attained after considerable practice, and perfect results are not to be expected at the outset.

But initial mistakes can easily be made good, for the colour can be washed off again. Mistakes in colouring can be corrected by applying the opposite colour. If the colour applied turns out too light, it can be toned down by spraying over with a darker shade of colour. Never use pure black in such a case, but dilute it with white to give the correct shade of grey.

Mistakes may also be rectified by other retouching methods. Any surface showing signs of uneven spraying can be rubbed over with artist's chalk, and the detail strengthened with retouching crayons.

After a little experience, mistakes will become less frequent. These are the main points which must be observed if good results are to be obtained.

1. The air brush is a precision instrument. Always clean it immediately after use.

2. Never use anything but special air brush colours.

3. To obtain any desired tone, mix the correct shade, do not try to lighten or darken areas with white or black respectively.

4. It is better to apply too little colour than too much.

5. Allow the colour to dry after each coating before applying a second coat.

6. Before spraying a print, always test the air brush on a piece of paper.

7. Always keep to the recommended air pressure for the type of brush.

8. Do not dismantle the air brush except when absolutely necessary for cleaning purposes. With proper treatment it should never be necessary.

Cleaning after Use

After use, do not put off the cleaning until later, but rinse the brush at once and dry it out. The procedure is as follows :

Empty the colour cup so that no colour flows through the nozzle. With the aid of a dropping-tube fill the cup with water and rinse out by alternatively squirting and sucking a few times, afterwards removing all water by the same means.

Repeat the process until no trace of colour remains.

Finally fill the cup with water again and operate the brush so that water is prayed out. As the water emerges, carefully place the index finger over the orifice, taking care not to touch the nozzle and regulating needle. By thus closing the orifice the compressed air is made to pass from the nozzle into the cup. As it passes over the needle, it drives any colour that may still be adhering to it back into the cup.

Remove any remaining traces of colour from the cup with the dropping tube, and repeat the process until all parts of the instrument are clean. Lastly, blow the brush through with compressed air until the inside is quite dry.

RESTORING DAMAGED PICTURES

Negatives and prints are subject to deterioration and damage from careless processing and unsuitable storage. Various methods of treatment will often render them serviceable again.

Stains

Stains on negatives may arise from a number of different causes and it is impossible to lay down hard and fast rules for tracing the fault, which must be found by trial and error.

Whatever method is used to restore old negatives, there is always the risk of damage. If the negative is valuable or irreplaceable, it is therefore advisable to make a duplicate negative before starting treatment on the original. If the original is spoiled, a makeshift print can then be obtained from the retouched duplicate.

Negative stains will often yield to the following solution:

27.—STAIN REMOVER

Sodium thiosulphate	1½ ounces	40 grams
Water	4 ounces	100 c.cm.
Glycerine	4 ounces	100 c.cm.

Paint the solution repeatedly over the stains. If necessary the solution can be left on the emulsion for several days until the stains are bleached out.

The following bleaching bath provides an alternative method of removing stains :

28.—ALTERNATIVE STAIN REMOVER

Potassium bichromate	175 grains	10 grams
Hydrochloric acid (concentrated)	60 minims	3 c.cm.
Water	4 ounces	100 c.cm.

Leave the negative in the bath until the stains disappear. Then redevelop in a normal (*not* fine grain) negative or print developer, e.g., formula No. 35 on p. 188.

The following method of removing developer stains involves two successive bleaching baths, a clearing bath, rinsing and development. The baths are made up and the treatment proceeds as follows :

29.—FIRST BLEACHING BATH

Potassium bichromate	25 grains	1·5 grams
Sodium chloride	175 grains	10 grams
Sulphuric acid, 10% solution	4 ounces	100 c.cm.

Bleach the negative in the above solution. Rinse briefly, then transfer to :

30.—SECOND BLEACHING BATH

Potassium permanganate	45 grains	2·7 grams
Sulphuric acid, 10% solution	3½ ounces	85 c.cm.
Water to make	40 ounces	1,000 c.cm.

Through formation of manganese dioxide this bath turns the negative brown. Rinse for 10 minutes then transfer to :

31.—CLEARING BATH

Sodium sulphite, crystals	88 grains	5 grams
Sulphuric acid, 10% solution	1½ ounces	38 c.cm.
Water	40 ounces	1,000 c.cm.

Rinse for 30 minutes, then redevelop.

Water Spots

Spots on a negative caused by accidental wetting with water can only be removed by immediately leaving the negative to soak for some time in water, then drying again.

Old and Varnished Negatives

Before restoring old negatives, any varnish or dope must first be removed with alcohol.

The gelatine of old negatives tends to absorb moisture less readily and is less susceptible to chemical action. Before attempting any restoration work on an old negative, therefore, soak it in a weak solution of ammonia until the gelatine appears to have swollen sufficiently.

Restoring Prints

The danger of spoiling a print in the attempt to restore it is always present. Before starting work on a dirty or faded print it is therefore a wise precaution to copy it, so that if the worst happens, we have at least a duplicate of the print as it was before.

First remove any dust from the surface by rubbing with soft bread or a soft art eraser. Unlike normal indiarubber this does not attack the surface. Avoid undue friction as the static electricity generated thereby will attract dust instead of removing it.

Greasy dirt, e.g., finger-marks and the like, will usually disappear if carefully rubbed with either petrol, or carbon tetrachloride with 5 per cent ethylene trichloride added.

Marking ink can be removed by immersing the print in 1 per cent sodium bisulphite solution.

Ink spots will often bleach out in a 10 per cent solution of oxalic or citric acid.

Spots due to chemical action can be removed with the aid of the following bleaching bath :

32.—IODINE BLEACHER

Water	4 ounces	100 c.cm.
Potassium iodide	175 grains	10 grams
Iodine	20 grains	1 gram

For use, dilute one part of the solution with 100 parts of water.

Leave the print in the bath until the spots turn bluish. Rinse briefly and place in a fresh fixing bath, when the spots will disappear.

Faded Prints

There is no entirely reliable method of restoring faded prints, but the following two ways are often effective :

For the first method, soak the print thoroughly in a weak solution of ammonia until the paper swells slightly. Then place in the following bleaching bath :

33.—BICHROMATE BLEACHER

Potassium bichromate	55 grains	3 grams
Sodium chloride	55 grains	3 grams
Water	4 ounces	100 c.cm.
Hydrochloric acid, concentrated	40 minims	2 c.cm.

After immersion in the above bath, wash thoroughly and redevelop in normal developer.

The second method restores the silver in the image which had formed compounds and so caused discoloration. Wash the print, then place it in the following bleaching bath :

34.—COPPER SULPHATE BLEACHER

Copper sulphate	18 grains	1 gram
Sodium chloride	90 grains	5 grams
Water	4 ounces	100 c.cm.

When bleached out, wash very thoroughly, then redevelop in vigorous developer. The following formula is recommended.

35.—METOL-HYDROQUINONE DEVELOPER

Metol	90 grains	5 grams
Sodium sulphite, crystals	3¼ ounces	80 grams
Hydroquinone	110 grains	6 grams
Potassium carbonate	1½ ounces	40 grams
Potassium bromide	110 grains	6 grams
Water to make	40 ounces	1,000 c.cm.

This developer is used undiluted.

Instead of the above developer, a solution of sodium stannate also gives good results. This is prepared by taking a 1 per cent solution of stannous chloride and adding a 10 per cent solution of caustic soda in sufficient quantity to dissolve the initial precipitate.

After treatment the print should be thoroughly rinsed.

INDEX

A

Abrasive medium 91, 110
Abrasive powders and pastes
107, 108, 110
Abrasive retouching 54, 91–92, 106–117
Abrasive stumps ... 91, 106, 107
Acid, to neutralize 160
Air brush, cleaning an 183
Air brush, colours 166, 168
Air brushes 162, 165–7
Air brushing 131, 163, 165–84
Ammonia solution 16, 187, 188
Artificial light, retouching by ... 65
Atmospheric action, deterioration by 162
Atomizer 163

B

Bacteria 74
Bleaching ... 63, 64, 153, 157, 185, 188
Bleaching baths 153, 186–8
Blocking out 78, 102, 132–5
Brushes 88

C

Carbon tetrachloride ... 117, 136
Centre of negative, reducing 57, 58–9
Chalk, artist's ... 158, 159, 183
Chalk, black 158, 159
Chalk to neutralize acid 160
Chalk, white 158, 159
Cheeks 40
Chemical retouching 53, 54, 56–64, 81,
83, 154–7, 158–8
Chin 41, 47
Cleanliness 15–16
Clearing baths 156, 186
Clouds 58, 132, 182
Colour photography 132
Contrasty negatives 56, 70, 144, 153
Copying 51
Crayon 145, 158, 183
Crayon, oil 155, 159
Cut-outs 150

D

Daylight, retouching by 65
Density 54, 56, 57, 58, 126, 127, 144,
153, 179

Desk, retouching ... 65–9, 84, 85, 178
Dust ... ... 15, 76, 140 ,151
Duto 49
Dye retouching 53, 54, 68, 70–80, 90,
105, 133, 134, 141, 149, 155, 157–61

E

Ears 48
Electric charge ... 15, 16, 187
Enlarging 16, 78, 111, 116, 122, 123, 129,
132, 136, 141, 142, 143, 161
Eyes 36–9

F

Film backing, matt ... 55, 73, 120, 131
Film, choosing 22–3, 49
Film, double-coated 55
Film, infra-red 51
Film, miniature 16, 55, 58, 74, 103, 129,
136, 139, 141, 142, 140, 144
Film, orthochromatic ... 22, 24, 49
Film, panchromatic ... 23, 25, 49, 50
Filters, pale green 49
Filters, polarizing 50
Finger-print marks 16, 17, 141, 161, 187
Forehead 44, 45
Freckles 22, 23

G

Gelatine layer 16, 58, 71, 72, 74, 75, 78,
80, 105, 108, 141, 187
Glycerine 135
Gradation, remedying flat 161
Grain, suppressing
139, 141, 142, 143, 144, 153
Graphite, holding back with ...130–1
Grey dye 73
Gum arabic 159, 160
Gum medium 79, 105

H

Hair 35, 40
Halo effect 131
Holding back
53, 70–4, 86, 87 ,130, 131, 141

189

Indian ink 79, 80, 105
Intensification 53, 54, 56, 62–4, 154
Intensifier, chromium 64
Intensifier, copper 64

K

Knifing 53, 54, 74, 94, 95, 106, 111–17,
130, 131, 146, 147, 157, 159, 160
Kodak Pola-Filter 50

L

Lighting, control of 20–2, 50
Lips 34
Liquid filter to modify lighting ... 68

M

Make-up 24–9, 49, 50
Marking ink, to remove 187
Masks ... 51, 111, 158, 176, 178–82
Materials for abrasive retouching
106, 107, 108, 110, 111, 112, 113
Materials for chemical retouching 56, 57
Materials for dye and pigment re-
touching ... 70, 73, 74, 75, 78, 161
Materials for pencil retouching
96, 120, 126, 127, 158
Matt effect 163
Metol-hydroquinone developer ... 188
Modulo 49
Mouth 32–4

N

Negative carrier, cleaning glass
plates of 16
Negatives, duplicate... 144
Negatives, handling 16, 57, 58
Negatives, storing 49
Neo-coccine 70, 129
Nose 43

O

Old negatives 185–7
Old prints 187–8
Opaques 75, 78
Outlines, sharp 59–60, 61, 111, 158, 179
Outlines, unsharp 60, 62, 63, 132–5, 182

P

Pencil retouching
53, 55, 96–100, 118–28, 141, 158, 160
Photo tints 161
Photo-montage 132

Pigment retouching
74, 79, 80, 105, 155, 157–ⁱ
Plates 16, 55, 71, 73, 129, 13ⁱ
Plates, broken ... 104, 137, 138
Position, working 56, 69, 85
Poster paint, white 158
Potassium metabisulphite bath 63, 64, 156
Preventing need for retouching 15–51
Printing paper, glossy 142, 157, 160–1
Printing paper, hard grade ... 70
Printing paper, matt 155, 157–9, 161
Printing paper, rough surfaced ... 142
Printing paper, semi-matt ... 159–61, 163
Prints, retouching 74, 154–64
Process white 158, 159

R

Red dye 70, 72
Redeveloper for fine grain ... 144, 153
Redevelopment 144, 153
Reducer, dry 108
Reducer, Farmer's 58, 156
Reducer, ferric oxalate 60
Reducer, potassium ferricyanide ... 62
Reducer, potassium permanganate... 156
Reduction 54, 56, 57, 58–62, 70, 82, 83,
154, 155, 156
Reproduction, retouching for 154, 158–64
Rolleisoft 49
Rubber solution, diluted, resist
medium 60

S

Scratches 136, 137, 138
Silver deposit 56, 106, 144, 156, 188
Skies, reduction of ... 57, 58, 81
Skies, dye retouching of 73
Skies, graininess of ... 141, 142
Skin blemishes 49, 50
Sodium stannate solution 188
Sodium sulphide 157
Sodium thiosulphate solution ... 62
Soft-focus attachment 49
Soft focus in enlarging ... 18, 142
Soft focus lens ... 19, 49–50, 51
Spotting
54, 74–80, 89, 105, 140, 148, 154, 157–61
Spray gun 163, 167
Spraying 163
Stains on old negatives 185
Stains, removing chemical 187
Stains, removing developer ... 186
Stains, removing ink 187
Stains, removing marking ink ... 187
Stains, removing yellow ... 155, 156
Starch solution 163

T

Teeth 32, 33
Thiocarbamide clearing bath 155, 156
Tinting 164

V

Varnish after knifing prints ... 159
Varnish, air brush masking ... 181
Varnish, carbon tetrachloride as substitute for 117
Varnish, cellulose 163
Varnish for pencil retouching 53, 55, 97, 120, 121, 122, 123, 125
Varnish for plates 129, 130
Varnish for scratches 138
Varnish, resist 60, 64, 71, 74, 117
Varnish, spraying 163
Varnish to restore gradation of prints 161–2
Varnish, Zapon 163
Vignetting effects 51

W

Water colour paints 53, 78, 79, 80, 105, 129, 131, 157, 161, 162, 163, 167, 168
Water marks, to remove 16, 49, 186
Waterproof coating 60
Wax polish for prints 162
Wetting agent 15
Wrinkles 46

Z

Zeiss Bernotar 50

COMPANION VOLUMES TO THIS MANUAL

DEVELOPING

The Technique of the Negative

By C. I. Jacobson, Ph.D.

80 photographs, 70 diagrams, 304 pages, 197 formulae, 39 tables, $7\frac{1}{2} \times 5$ inches, cloth bound. Price **15/6**. (Postage **6d**). Twelfth edition.

ENLARGING

The Technique of the Positive

By C. I. Jacobson, Ph.D.

58 photographs, 78 diagrams, 304 pages, 75 formulae, 33 tables, $7\frac{1}{2} \times 5$ inches, cloth bound. Price **15/6**. (Postage **6d**.)
Fourteenth edition

OPTICS

The Technique of Definition

By Arthur Cox, M.A., B.Sc.

360 diagrams, 35 tables, 368 pages, $7\frac{1}{2} \times 5$ inches, cloth bound. Price **17/6**. (Postage **6d**.)
Ninth edition

EXPOSURE

Fundamentals of Camera Technique

By W. F. Berg, D.Sc., Ph.D., F.R.P.S.

84 photographs, 56 diagrams, 432 pages, $7\frac{1}{2} \times 5$ inches, cloth bound. Price **21/-**. (Postage **6d**.)

ILLUMINATION

The Technique of Light

By R. Howard Cricks, F.R.P.S., F.B.K.S.

90 diagrams, 320 pages, $7\frac{1}{2} \times 5$ inches, cloth bound. Price **17/6**. (Postage **6d**.)

PHOTOGRAPHING PEOPLE

By Hugo van Wadenoyen, F.R.P.S.

Solemnly pictorial portraits have been replaced by candid records of people's faces. The new aims and the means to them are explained in this book.
168 pp., 189 illus., VIII ed. **Price 12/6**

STRAIGHTFORWARD DEVELOPING

By L. A. Mannheim

You need only a simple developing box and somebody to show you how. This book will do it.
96 pp., 150 illus., II ed. **Price 5/-**

LIGHTING FOR PHOTOGRAPHY

By W. Nurnberg, F.R.P.S.

The technical roots of artificial lighting, the advantages and limitations of different light sources, the principles of their practical use.
176 pp., 297 illus., XI ed. **Price 17/6**

PHOTOFLASH IN PRACTICE

By Geoffrey Gilbert

The flash bulb has become the most popular source of illumination both indoors and outdoors and under unfavourable lighting conditions.
256 pp., 96 illus., III ed. **Price 13/6**

FOCAL FLASH DISC

By W. D. Emanuel

For use with flash bulbs or speed flash ; gives correct exposure with any bulb, with any film, at any distance.
Price 5/-

35 mm. PHOTO TECHNIQUE

By H. S. Newcombe, F.R.P.S.

Technical factors of film, exposure and development producing the perfect negative are put into the language of common sense for the practical man.
320 pp., 90 illus., VII ed. **Price 17/6**

PHOTOGRAPHY AT SCHOOL AND COLLEGE

By M. K. Kidd

Written for active but impecunious young people, showing short cuts to successful photography and dealing especially with the subjects that interest them.
200 pp., 211 illus. **Price 7/6**

LANDSCAPE PHOTOGRAPHY

By Leonard and Marjorie Gayton

The Gaytons show how to put the landscape first and the camera second, to picture mood as much as a view.
160 pp., 44 illus. **Price 25/-**

THE COMPLETE ART OF PRINTING AND ENLARGING

By O. R. Croy

How to make prints—ordinary prints, elaborately controlled or very tricky prints ; a wealth of technical knowledge and personal experience.
256 pp., 200 illus., III ed. **Price 19/6**

STRAIGHTFORWARD PRINT MAKING

By L. A. Mannheim

Making your own prints is a simple job. Turn out perfect pictures every time without bother or elaborate equipment.
96 pp., 200 lilus., II ed. **Price 5/-**

LIGHTING FOR PORTRAITURE

By W. Nurnberg, F.R.P.S.

With extreme clarity and profuse illustrations, the author of Lighting for Photography here describes the manifold possibilities of lighting the human face.
192 pp., 240 illus., II ed. **Price 17/6**

MEDICAL PHOTOGRAPHY

By T. A. Longmore, A.R.P.S., M.S.R.

The photographic background on which the radiographic and the clinic cameraworker rely. Strictly factual and exhaustive.
1012 pp., 440 illus., IV ed. **Price 50/-**

FOCAL EXPOSURE DISC

By W. D. Emanuel

Presents reliable results ready for reading off at a glance just as the best types of exposure meters would do.
Price 5/-

TWIN-LENS COMPANION

By H. S. Newcombe, F.R.P.S.

Contributions on their twin-lens technique by ten American professional photographers of world-wide fame complement advice to beginner and advanced worker.
320 pp., 90 illus., II ed. **Price 17/6**

ALL THE PHOTO TRICKS

By Edwin Smith

Shows how startling pictorial effects, fantastic variations of reality, amusing deceptions of the eye and even political propaganda are worked through photography.
280 pp., 147 illus., IV ed. **Price 15/6**

ALL-IN-ONE-CAMERA BOOK

By W. D. Emanuel

The easy path to good photography is shown as a pleasant hobby with a technical background—the problems are simplified but not concealed.
232 pp., 80 illus., XXVIII ed. **Price 9/6**

100,000 EXPOSURES
By E. O. Hoppe
In this blend of personal memoirs, technical instructions and business advice, the first of all camera aces looks back and shows what he has learned and seen.
226 pp., 70 illus., IV ed.   **Price 13/6**

MY WAY WITH THE MINIATURE
By Lancelot Vining
Ten years more experience has gone into the thorough revision, ample additions and new illustrations of the present re-issue of this work.
260 pp., 50 illus., X ed.   **Price 15/6**

AMATEUR CARBRO COLOUR PRINTS
By Viscount Hanworth
Shows how to do a first-rate job with amateur means. The author, an amateur himself, gives detailed, step by step explanations.
160 pp., 33 illus., II ed.   **Price 12/6**

COLOUR TRANSPARENCIES
By C. Leslie Thomson, B.Sc.
The *Handbooks of Colour Photography* supply theory, technical data, practical advice. This book is devoted to the most popular and recent processes.
296 pp., 60 illus.   **Price 17/6**

PHOTOGRAPHS AND THE PRINTER
By Frank H. Smith
This book tells how and why and what sort of photographs will give the best results when printed by the printer.
176 pp., 62 illus.   **Price 12/6**

THE ROLLEI WAY
By L. A. Mannheim
A composite work, built from the experience and advice of leading photographers, dealing with essential points of Rolleiflex or Rolleicord practice.
232 pp., 245 illus., II ed.   **Price 17/6**

MAKING LANTERN SLIDES AND FILMSTRIPS
By C. Douglas Milner
This book sorts out the best from traditional experience and combines it with the results of modern research.
224 pp., 85 illus., II ed.   **Price 12/6**

BUSINESS OF PHOTOGRAPHY
By Charles Ash
The author is the Executive Manager of the Photographers' Association of America. A British running commentary adds a world-wide usefulness to the book.
416 pp.   **Price 16/6**

LIVING ON MY CAMERA
By J. Allan Cash
A roving free-lance photographer, beginning without much means or experience, shows what pictures he took, the way he sold them and what he got out of it.
268 pp., 78 illus., II ed.   **Price 15/-**

WITHOUT ASSIGNMENT
By Howard Byrne
The author's camera adventures in Europe and the United States reveal a vast amount of " know-how " about free-lance photo-journalism.
200 pp., 70 illus.   **Price 17/6**

THE TECHNIQUE OF FILM EDITING
Compiled by Karel Reisz
Ten outstanding film editors summarise their views and experience and present the first comprehensive guide to their craft.
288 pp., 189 illus.   **Price 30/-**

MAKING COLOUR PRINTS
By Jack H. Coote, F.R.P.S.
The print-making processes described in a simple but comprehensive manner, and graded according to ease of working.
128 pp., 64 illus., XVI ed.   **Price 7/6**

THE CONTAX WAY
By H. Freytag
Up-to-date facts and authoritative advice on all Contax equipment applied to every conceivable Contax subject.
224 pp., 241 illus., III ed.   **Price 17/6**

THE RETINA WAY
By O. R. Croy
Will put the whole Retina technique safely in your hands and bring all the subjects of Retina photography within your easy reach.
240 pp., 214 illus., II ed.   **Price 17/6**

FILMSTRIP AND SLIDE PROJECTION
By M. K. Kidd and C. W. Long
How to choose your projector, set it up and handle its electrical factors ; fit up projection rooms ; make a projector.
160 pp., 62 illus.   **Price 7/6**

FOTOJOB BOOKS
Written by professionals. *Wedding Photography*, by Gordon Catling ; *Group Photography*, by Gordon Catling ; *Photographing Machinery*, by Bernard Alfieri.
96–112 pp., 32–43 illus.   **Each 7/6**

PHOTOGRAPHY AS A CAREER
Edited by A. Kraszna-Krausz
Twenty photographers, all masters of their craft, give personal opinions and advice as to how newcomers should approach their fields of work.
208 pp., 12 diags., III ed.　　**Price 12/6**

WORKING FOR THE FILMS
Ed. by Oswell Blakeston
Personal stories and frank opinions of twenty celebrated protagonists of British films contain honest advice and all needed warning on films as a career.
208 pp., 2-colour illus.　　**Price 10/6**

PHOTOGRAPHERS' GUIDE TO BRITAIN
It points the way to many interesting photo subjects ; it shows how to get the best effects with the weather and the light ; it suggests the right technique.
224 pp.　　**Price 7/6**

CAMERA IN PARIS
By Brassai
Brassai's photographic equipment is more modest than that of many an advanced amateur, yet his photographs of Paris created a new style and a new approach.
96 pp., 64 illus.　　**Price 15/6**

MOUNTAIN PHOTOGRAPHY
By C. Douglas-Milner
The only comprehensive English work based on thorough photographic research and rich mountaineering experience.
232 pp., 222 illus., II ed.　　**Price 19/6**

PHOTO-WORDS IN FOUR LANGUAGES
Whether you know the English word and want its equivalent in French, German or Spanish, or the other way round, the answer is here.
64 pp.　　**Price 3/6**

NATURE AND CAMERA
By Oliver G. Pike, F.R.P.S., F.I.B.P.
Sums up fifty years' experience and shows how nature photography is just a blend of the right approach and a few simple " tricks."
264 pp., 193 illus., VI ed.　　**Price 13/6**

AMATEURS JUST LIKE YOU
Six leading amateurs tell how they became interested in their own fields and illustrate their methods.
212 pp., 45 illus.　　**Price 15/6**

PHOTOMICROGRAPHY
By Alan Jackson, B.Sc., A.I.C.
The methods and equipment used in photomicrography, an interesting hobby as much as a scientific technique.
184 pp., 68 illus., VI ed.　　**Price 8/6**

DOCUMENT PHOTOGRAPHY
By H. W. Greenwood
The first modern comprehensive survey of cameras and accessories available, with instructions for their use.
164 pp., 52 illus., III ed.　　**Price 7/6**

PROGRESS IN PHOTOGRAPHY
Edited by D. A. Spencer
Records the significant advances made in scientific research and technological development applied to photography all over the world during the last ten years.
464 pp.　　**Price 42/-**

PHOTO-AMATEUR'S POCKETBOOK
This handy, fact-crammed pocket-full gives top value in photographic literature: photographs by masters, advice on seasonable subjects, diary section, register for data, condensed technical reference library.
312 pp.　　**Price 5/-**

MARKET FOR PHOTOGRAPHS
How to get your pictures published. A comprehensive directory setting out the types of pictures editors want, their terms of payment, etc.
224 pp.　　**Price 10/6**

UNFORGETTABLE SNAPSHOTS
By Hugo van Wadenoyen
To-day, even the simplest cameras will take pictures as good as those taken by the most expensive outfits some time ago.
32 pp., 27 illus.　　**Price 1/-**

FOCAL CINE BOOKS

HOW TO FILM *by G. Wain*
Make sure that your pictures will come out sharp, are well exposed, are the right length and make sense without having to explain them.

HOW TO PROJECT *by Norman Jenkins*
The choice of the right projector, the right screen, the right seating plan can mean the crowning triumph of a production.

HOW TO USE 9.5 mm. FILM *by D. M. Neale*
Ideas, experience and advice for everyone who wants to make films that will not cost more than taking a few snaps.

HOW TO MAKE HOLIDAY FILMS *by H. Baddeley*
Whether your holiday is afloat or ashore, at home or abroad, lazy or energetic, you will find here how to make a successful film out of it.

HOW TO USE COLOUR *by C. Leslie Thomson*
What materials to choose, how to expose without fail, how to make the best of the lighting outdoors, how to set up lights indoors.

HOW TO TITLE *by L. F. Minter*
How to design and layout a title, how to draw or paint it, how to photograph it, how to fit it into your film to tie together the sequences.

HOW TO EDIT *by H. Baddeley*
By following a few simple rules and with a little skill, film editing will suggest time, bridge space, fill in detail, lend emphasis, change speed.

HOW TO SCRIPT *by Oswell Blakeston*
Read here how to translate a thought into a picture and how to string cine shots into a story that flows.
160 pages, fully illustrated. **Price 7/6 each** (Postage 6d.)

HOW TO DIRECT *by Tony Rose*
The amateur film director must get his film finished within a narrow time schedule, keep an eye on running length, ensure proper continuity of action, put emphasis where emphasis belongs.

HOW TO PROCESS *by Leslie Wheeler*
If you can process ordinary roll film you are but a step from processing cine film. How to do it with very little equipment.

HOW TO CAERTOON *by J. Hales and B. Privett*
Cartoon films are easy magic : a mere matter of paints, brush and scissors, and the simplest camera technique.

HOW TO ACT *by Tony Rose and Martin Benson*
Every move and gesture of the film actor must be suited to the requirements of the camera, while still making his performance credible.
160 pages, fully illustrated. **Price 6/- each** (Postage 3d.)

THE CINE ALMANAC
Contains a wide range of feature articles, all the technical data a cine enthusiast needs, and directories of film libraries and cine clubs.
232 pages. **Price 15/6** (Postage 6d.)

THE focal PHOTO GUIDES

The Most Popular Photographic Library in the World ; 2/- each

1   All About FOCUSING and Your Camera, by F. W. Frerk
2   All About SUNSHINE and Your Camera, by Edwin Smith
3   All About FILTERS and Your Camera, by C. I. Jacobson
4   All About PORTRAITS and Your Camera, by Hugo van Wadenoyen
5   All About EXPOSURE and Your Camera, by C. I. Jacobson
6   All About TAKING ACTION with Your Camera, by Alex. Strasser
7   All About LANDSCAPES and Your Camera, by Hugo van Wadenoyen
8   All About FORMULAE in Your Darkroom, by C. I. Jacobson
9   All About DAYLIGHT INDOORS and Your Camera, by Hugo van Wadenoyen
10 All About IMPROVING NEGATIVES in Your Darkroom, by F. W. Frerk
11 All About WINTER PHOTOGRAPHY and Your Camera, by Edwin Smith
12 All About TRACING TROUBLES in Your Photographs, by A. Merryweather
13 All About LIGHTING WITH ONE LAMP and Your Camera, by H. Van Wadenoyen
14 All About LIGHTING WITH TWO LAMPS, by Hugo van Wadenoyen
15 All About COMPOSITION and Your Camera, by A. Kraszna-Krausz
16 All About IMPROVING PRINTS in Your Darkroom, by F. W. Frerk
17 All about AGAINST THE SUN EFFECTS and Your Camera, by Hugo van Wadenoyen
18 All About PHOTOS IN YOUR GARDEN and Your Camera, by R. M. Fanstone
19 All About COPYING and Your Camera, by H. W. Ggreenwood
20 All About MAKING ENLARGEMENTS in Your Darkroom, by C. I. Jacobson
21 All About PROCESSING in Your Darkroom, by C. I. Jacobson
22 All About ARCHITECTURE and Your Camera, by R. M. Fanstone
23 All About SELLING PHOTOGRAPHS, by Bernard Alfieri
24 All About SPORTS AND GAMES and Your Camera, by Lancelot Vining
25 All About PICTURES IN TOWN and Your Camera, by Hugo van Wadenoyen
26 All About CHILDREN OUTDOORS and Your Camera, by Hugo van Wadenoyen
27 All About CAMERAS and How to Choose Yours, by Bernard Alfieri
28 All About CATS AND KITTENS and Your Camera, by Philip Johnson
29 All About DOGS AND PUPPIES adn Your Camera, by Philip Johnson
30 All About CHILDREN INDOORS and Yours Camera, by Hugo van Wadenoyen
31 All About MOTHER AND CHILD PICTURES and Your Camera, by T. P. H. Miller
32 All About LIGHTING FOR GLAMOUR and Your Camera, by W. Nurnberg
33 All About FLASH PHOTOGRAPHY and Your Camera, by F. W. Frerk
34 All About NIGHT PHOTOGRAPHY and Your Camera, by F. Purves
35 All About MAKING CONTACT PRINTS from Your Negatives, by Betti Mautner
36 All About USING A MINIATURE CAMERA, by Percy W. Harris
37 All About TAKING WEDDINGS with Your Camera, by Gordon Catilng
38 All About TAKING BABY and Your Camera, by W. Suschitzky
39 All About PRINT FINISHING, by R. M. Fanstone
40 All About TAKING COLOUR, by C. L. Thomson
41 All About COLOUR OUTDOORS, by George Wells
42 All About COLOUR INDOORS, by George Wells
43 All About PORTRAITS IN COLOUR, by George Wells
44 All About BUILDING YOUR OWN ENLARGER, by Gordon Catling
45 All About MAKING CAMERA GADGETS, by L. C. Mason
46 All About PROCESSING 35 mm. FILM, by Percy W. Harris
47 All About TAKING PARTIES AND GROUPS, by Gordon Catling
48 All About PICTURES IN THE HILLS, by C. Douglas Milner
49 All About MAKING LIGHTING GADGETS, by L. C. Mason
50 All About TRAVELLING with Your Camera, by Edward Richardson
51 All About PHOTOGRAPHING SHOWS, by Angus Wilson
52 All About TAKING GREAT OCCASIONS, with Your Camera, by Gordon Catling
53 All About GLAMOUR IN COLOUR, by George Wells
54 All About CHILDREN IN COLOUR, by George Wells
55 All About FLASH AND COLOUR, by George Wells
56 All About YOUR HOLIDAYS IN COLOUR, by George Wells

FOCAL CHARTS

FOCAL DEVELOPING CHART
By W. D. Emanuel

The right developing time at any temperature.

FOCAL EXPOSURE CHART
By W. D. Emanuel

Anywhere, any time, any subject, any light, any camera, any film.

FOCAL FILTER CHART
By W. D. Emanuel

The right filter, the right film, the right light, the right stop.

FOCAL FOCUSING CHART
By Arthur Cox

Sharp focus, safe depth, with any lens or attachment.

FOCAL LIGHTING CHART
By W. D. Emanuel

Simple lighting schemes, tested lamp positions, exact exposure.

FOCAL STOP AND SPEED CHART
By E. Steffens

A whole library of facts on exposure, depth and action.

FOCAL FLASH CHART
By W. D. Emanuel

Flash exposure disc, sun-flash exposure disc, ten typical set-ups.

FOCAL CINE CHART
By W. D. Emanuel

All the technical data needed.

Price 3/6 each (Postage 3d.)

FOCAL ENLARGING CHART
By W. D. Emanuel

Measures exposures, ensures sharpness, defines magnification.

Price 7/6 (Postage 6d.)

PHOTO PAMPHLETS

MAKING AN ENLARGER
DEPTH OF FOCUS

Price 3/6 each (Po tage 3d.)

CAMERA GUIDES

BOLEX GUIDE
By A. J. Surgenor

Price 7/6 (Postage 6d.)

LEICA GUIDE
By W. D. Emanuel

ROLLEIFLEX GUIDE
By W. D. Emanuel

EXAKTA GUIDE
By W. D. Emanuel

CONTAX GUIDE
By W. D. Emanuel

Price 6/6 each (Postage 3d.)

ROBOT GUIDE
By W. D. Emanuel

Price 5/6 (Postage 3d.)

KORELLE GUIDE
By W. D. Emanuel

IKONTA GUIDE
By W. D. Emanuel

RETINA GUIDE
By W. D. Emanuel

SELFIX GUIDE
By W. D. Emanuel

VITO GUIDE
By W. D. Emanuel

PURMA GUIDE
By Frederick Purves

VITESSA GUIDE
By W. D. Emanuel

ISOLETTE GUIDE
By W. D. Emanuel

KARAT GUIDE
By W. D. Emanuel

NETTAR GUIDE
By W. D. Emanuel

CONTESSA GUIDE
By W. D. Emanuel

Price 4/6 each (Postage 3d.)

FUL-VUE GUIDE
By Marcel Natkin

Price 2/6 (Postage 3d.)

PHOTOGUIDE MAGAZINE

the best

monthly

If you like the Photo Guides you will like the PhotoGuide Magazine even more. It is more lively and interesting than anything you have seen before.

Packed with the world's best photographs, drawings that make their point clear and a wide choice of reading matter.

You will find what you want; information and advice, experience and entertainment. All of it useful and never boring.

Photography is meant to be fun. The PhotoGuide Magazine is fun. It will help you to get more fun out of your camera—whatever camera you have.

The PhotoGuide Magazine keeps its feet firmly planted on the ground and yet it will fire your imagination. It will train your eye to find better pictures and help to improve your technique in getting them.

The PhotoGuide Magazine is worth every penny you pay for it and a lot more.

Is. 6d.

Subscription for a whole year **20s.** post free.

Write for free specimen copy.

PUBLISHED BY
31, FITZROY SQ.

FOCAL PRESS
LONDON, W.1